LIVING
JESUS

Growing In The LIFE
We Were Made To LIVE

Christian Families Today

A Christian Counseling and Training Ministry

ACKNOWLEDGEMENTS

The Snowman Diagrams (pages 9, 34, 55, 87, 110) and the Relationship Diagrams (pages 15, 21, 36, 40, and 56) were created by Greg and Connie Brezina and illustrated by Ben Brezina. CFT is a member of the Network 220 (www.network220.org). Some diagrams and content in this publication have been adapted from Network 220 conference materials.

Scripture quotations are taken from the New American Standard Bible®,
Copyright © 1960, 1962, 1963, 1968, 1971, 1972, 1973,
1975, 1977, 1995 by The Lockman Foundation
Used by permission. (www.Lockman.org)

Authors: Ben Brezina, Mark Fields, Tom Price, Greg Cleland
Editors: Greg Brezina, Beau Brezina, Connie Brezina, Jamie Pharis Pyles, Ross O'Hair
Designer & Illustrator: Ben Brezina

COPYRIGHT

Christian Families Today
174 Ashley Park Blvd STE 1, Newnan, GA 30263
Phone: 770-502-8050
E-mail: cft@CFTministry.org
www.ChristianFamiliesToday.org

Living IN Jesus Participant's Guide - 2nd Edition
ISBN: 978-0-9773660-6-4

CONTENTS

INTRODUCTION

"I have come that they might have life, and have it abundantly"

Jesus (John 10:10b)

You have probably heard the phrase "the gospel of Jesus Christ" if you have spent any time in a Christian church. The word "gospel" means good news. What is this news about Jesus Christ? What makes it so good?

If you were to ask these questions to a sample of Christians today, you would probably hear the news that Jesus died on the cross for the sins of the world. You also might hear the news that by placing your faith and trust in Jesus, you can escape hell and enjoy heaven forever with God. While these bits of news are very exciting and are wonderful parts of the gospel, they are merely prologue and post script. The main body of the good, glad, happy news of Jesus Christ is the abundant life He offers right now to all who believe.

The whole story of God's interaction with mankind is about life: God is it; Adam and Eve were given it; by sinning, they lost it; none of their descendants could re-access it; God promised to restore it; Christ came to give it; by faith we accept it; and moment by moment we now walk in it.

God is life, and He designed all humans to operate in His life. As humans, we experience abundant life by having a personal relationship and intimate fellowship with the God of life. When His Spirit is living in us and we are enjoying His presence, we experience love, joy, peace, satisfaction, and fulfillment even in the midst of life's stress, pain, and trials.

Jesus once said that the greatest commandment is to love God with all your heart and the second greatest is to love your neighbor as you love yourself. The life of Christ is the only thing that makes obeying these commandments possible. God is love, and His life in us empowers us to love Him, love ourselves, and love others. Living out of His life is the only real way to experience internal health and relational harmony.

PURPOSE

The purpose of this study is life transformation. Our desire is for all believers to understand who God is, who they are in Christ, and how to live out of Christ's life on a moment-by-moment basis during their time on this earth.

For this reason, we focus on the abundant life of God throughout all sessions. The study starts by looking at God, who is the source of life. We then systematically look at how humanity was created for abundant life, how that life was lost, and how God restored life. In the remaining sessions, we discover how we can experience His abundant life moment by moment right now in our personal lives and social interactions.

Each session is a stepping-stone to the next. As such, we designed the sessions to be completed in order. Our journey leads us into the mechanics of what broke in Adam and Eve. From there we gain an understanding of the work Jesus needed to accomplish, so that He might give His life back to us. We talk about the old identity and the new identity, as well as the old covenant and the new covenant. Many Biblical truths are referenced and discussed to guide us into a practical understanding of how to experience Christ's abundant life while we are living here on earth. To help us conceptualize these spiritual truths, we have included many illustrations that we use daily in our discipleship counseling and coaching at Christian Families Today. It is going to be fun!

INTRODUCTION

IS THIS STUDY FOR ME?

Everyone can benefit from this study.

Maybe you are just starting to explore the Bible and want to know about Jesus and what He offers. This study will show you clearly what Jesus came to do and will describe the wonderful abundant life He offers you.

Maybe you are a young believer who wants to grow more in knowledge about what happened to you when you were saved. A person who is born again spiritually can be compared to a baby who will grow to maturity. This course will give you a great foundation of who you are now in Christ and how to experience victory over your enemy, Satan.

Maybe you have followed Christ for some time now. When you surrendered to Christ and trusted Him as your Lord and Savior, you may have thought the "abundant life" would be blissfully experienced all the time. At first, that may have been your experience, but after a short while, the struggle began. You may have had questions such as, "Why do I keep committing the same sin over and over again?" or "Why can't I be good enough?" or "What is wrong with me?" Many Christians struggle with these inner conflicts. This course is designed to help you answer those questions and to give you the truth you need to fight the lies you face.

Maybe you are a mature believer who has walked intimately with God for many years. If so, you know good news never gets old. We all benefit greatly from feeding on the truth every day. This course may present things in a different way than you have heard before. It could be like looking at the same diamond from a different angle. The beauty of the gospel may shine forth in a new way for you.

Wherever you find yourself in life, our prayer is that this study will lead you to experience more freedom, more health, and more wholeness through deeper intimacy with God. May He amaze you with His grace, kindness, power, and generosity toward you in Christ. We pray the time you invest in this course will help you practically as you seek to express the life of God to those around you.

ENJOY THE JOURNEY OF LIVING IN JESUS...

HOW TO USE THIS BOOK

While you may benefit from going through this book by yourself, "Living in Jesus" is not designed to be a stand-alone learning experience. It is specifically designed to be used together with another person or a small group of people. To this end, we have divided each session into four sections:

CONNECT

Each session will begin with a time to connect with the other person/people. As your time together begins, the first question in this section gives you a chance to share experiences or revelations since your last time together. Then, the questions will lead you into a short conversation about the topic for the day. It may also be good to use this opening time to build on the last session by reviewing together the "Transform" section from your last session.

RENEW

This section contains the content of the session and is designed to renew the mind through studying and meditating on the truths of God's word. The truths found in each session are organized under subheadings. Our hope is that you will both read through the information and then discuss each subheading. When you come to a question, take time to answer it before moving on. Conversation and interaction on the content will assist greatly in moving from simply knowing to truly believing the truths. Visual illustrations are provided to aid understanding. (A "Guide To Illustrations" is included at the back of the book.) This section is purposely filled with scriptures and references so you can trace everything back to God's written Word. We encourage you to take the time to look up the references so you will be like the noble-minded Bereans in Acts 17:10-11.

TRANSFORM

This third section gives an opportunity to individually process the session's truths. Each person should answer the questions individually and spend time in conversation with the Holy Spirit to allow Him to move the truths studied from information to transformation. Space is provided to record answers and thoughts, but feel free to use your own additional paper, if needed, to continue journaling as the Holy Spirit leads. As time allows, share your thoughts with the other person(s).

PRAY

We have included prayers at the end of every session to stimulate your conversation with God about His truths which are covered in each session. Our prayers are not magical. Praying is just a two-way conversation between you and God. You may use these prayers as a guide, but feel free to talk with God about whatever the Spirit is placing on your heart and then listen for what He wants to say to you. We encourage you to pray both individually and together with the person/people in your study.

CONCEPT OF GOD
Life

 ## CONNECT

- How would you describe God?

- How did you come to believe that?

- How would you go about finding out what God is really like?

 ## RENEW

GOD IS ETERNAL LIFE

God IS life (1 John 5:20). He does not contain life as a supplementary feature to His nature or character. He is the definition and source of eternal life. When God gives life, He is giving Himself (Ps. 36:9; John 6:63a; 1 John 1:2; 5:11-12).

God has no beginning and no end (Is. 46:10; Rev. 22:13). Eternal life, however, is more than the concept of infinite time. Time, as we conceive it, consists of past, present, and future. God is not bound by time (Gen. 1:1; John 1:1-2), as indicated by the name, "I AM," which God revealed to Moses (Ex. 3:14). He is an ever-present Now. God interacts with time because we presently live in time, but He exists outside of time.

"Jesus said to him, 'I am the way, and the truth, and the life; no one comes to the Father but through Me.'"
- John 14:6

GOD IS SPIRIT

The Bible says God is spirit (John 4:24). He is infinite and uncontained. This means we cannot comprehend God by incorporating our physical senses.

The Biblical word for spirit is "pneuma" in the Greek language and "ruach" in the Hebrew language. They both mean "a current of air" (i.e. breath or wind).

How can we know God without having the opportunity to physically see Him, hear Him, or touch Him? The Bible says God made Himself known to man through the Person of Jesus, who demonstrated God's full character and nature for us in the flesh during His earthly ministry (John 1:1, 14, 18; Phil. 2:6-8a; Col. 1:15a; 2:9).

We can know what God is like by looking at Jesus through the spiritual eyes of faith (John 14:7-9; Heb. 1:3a). Jesus expressed God's character and nature during His earthly ministry. We can gain an appreciation of God's character and nature by reading the Gospels, which act as a witness documenting the life of Jesus.

GOD IS LOVE

"In this is love, not that we loved God, but that He loved us and sent His Son to be the propitiation for our sins." - 1 John 4:10

What does "God is love" mean? The very essence of God is LOVE. Love is not something God "has." Love is something God "is" (1 John 4:8b).

Jesus demonstrated God's love in His life (Col. 1:19). God's love is not a feeling but a choice to always act in the best interest of another. God's love is unconditional, benevolent, graceful, merciful, and persistent (John 15:13; 1 Cor. 13:4-7).

Unconditional: God's nature is to love everyone (John 3:16). It is impossible for God not to love. For this reason, He even loves those who hate Him (Matt. 23:37; Rom. 5:8, 10).

Benevolent: God's love is selfless and sacrificial. He has a sincere concern for our welfare (Phil. 2:3-5; 1 John 4:9-10).

Graceful: Grace is God giving us what we do not deserve, His unmerited favor. We cannot earn God's grace, only receive it. The only requirement to receive God's grace is to be in relationship with Him, by faith in Jesus and what He accomplished on our behalf on the cross (Rom. 3:24; Eph. 2:5, 8).

Merciful: Mercy is God withholding from us what we deserve. God is both tender-hearted and compassionate toward His children (Ps. 103:10; Rom. 6:23; Eph. 2:4).

Persistent: God had us in mind before the foundation of the world and has always been pursuing us with His "lovingkindness" (Ps. 136; Jer. 31:3; Lam. 3:22-24; Eph. 1:4; 2 Tim. 2:13; Heb. 13:5).

GOD IS CREATOR

"In the beginning God created the heavens and the earth." - Genesis 1:1

The Bible says everything that exists comes from God's wisdom, imagination, and power (Gen. 1:1; Neh. 9:6; Prov. 3:19; Col. 1:16a). Creation testifies to this fact (Ps. 19:1; Rom. 1:20; Rev. 4:11).

God possesses certain attributes that enable Him to create and sustain His creation according to His word and purpose (Heb. 1:3).

- **God is all-knowing** (Ps. 147:5; Is. 46:9b-10). He knows all things at once. He has always known everything and will always know everything.

- **God is all-powerful** (Job 42:2; Jer. 32:17; Luke 1:37). He is without limitation, and nothing is too difficult for Him.

- **God is all-present** (Ps. 139:7; Jer. 23:24). He is present everywhere at every time because He is uncontained.

GOD IS RELATER

God is a Trinity. His life is the perfect example of relationship. God is One (Deut. 6:4; John 10:30), consisting of three distinct Persons - Father, Son, and Holy Spirit (Matt. 28:19). The Old Testament states that God is a relational being comprised of more than one Person (Gen. 1:26a; 3:22). Before creation, God enjoyed a harmonious loving relationship with Himself (within the Persons of the Godhead) (John 17:22-24).

In His life-time, Jesus demonstrated God as a relator (John 14:9; Col. 2:9). Out of His intimate union with the Father, Jesus pursued personal human relationships during His earthly ministry (John 4:34; 8:42; 10:30; 12:49; 14:31a).

Jesus loved His disciples. During the last three years of His life, He devoted most of His time to the twelve disciples (John 13:1). The Bible indicates that during His earthly ministry, Jesus was especially close to Peter, James, and John (Mark 9:2).

God created humanity so that they might know Him and enjoy a personal relationship and intimate fellowship with Him (Phil. 3:8). The Bible describes eternal life in terms of relationship (John 17:3).

NOTE: There are many more qualities and attributes of God mentioned in the Scriptures. A great book for further study on God and His attributes is *Knowledge of the Holy* by A.W. Tozer.

ILLUSTRATION: GOD IS A TRINITY

SUMMARY

God is life, spirit, and love. He is also the creator and the personal relater. All He creates flows from His essence. Knowing and possessing God's character and nature are essential to experiencing a personal relationship and intimate fellowship with Him.

TRANSFORM

Typically, our concept of God develops during our formative years. We often project onto God an image that reflects the character of the authority figures in our lives like parents, teachers, etc. Our concept may also be influenced by misguided religious teaching.

1. How did authority figures and/or religious teaching shape my concept of God in my formative years?

    _____

    _____

    _____

    _____

    _____

    _____

2. Has my concept of God changed? If so, what influences have shaped my present concept of God?

    _____

    _____

    _____

    _____

    _____

    _____

    _____

3. What attribute of God comforts me the most? Why?

    _____

    _____

    _____

    _____

    _____

    _____

4. Which of His attributes do I have trouble embracing? Why?

_____

_____

_____

_____

_____

_____

_____

5. What does a personal relationship and intimate fellowship with God look like to me?

_____

_____

_____

_____

_____

_____

_____

_____

 **PRAY**

Thank You, Father, for creating me and pursuing me with Your unconditional love and acceptance. I renounce the false impressions I have maintained about You and celebrate that You are my Heavenly Father who deeply loves me. I now know You have my best interest in mind and are continually working all things for my good. Regardless of what I feel or do, You will never leave me nor forsake me. As I grow in my understanding and appreciation for who You are, my love for You grows. My greatest desire, above all else, is to know You and to experience intimate fellowship with You. You are worthy, and I worship You. Amen.

DESIGN OF HUMANITY
Containers of Life

CONNECT

- What has God revealed to you since we last met?

- What is a human being?

- What are the components of a human being?

- Who are you? Describe yourself in three sentences.

RENEW

HUMANITY'S IDENTITY IS ESTABLISHED

If you were to go back in time to the garden of Eden and ask Adam to describe who he is, what answer might you receive? He might tell you that he is a tender of a garden. However, that would not be correct because that is simply his job and not his core identity. Adam might tell you he is a husband, but that title is a description of the relationship he possesses with Eve. To get to the core of Adam's identity, it is necessary to go back to the elemental way in which he was made. Looking at the manner in which he was created, Adam is a living being with a spirit and a soul, who resides inside a physical body made from dust (Gen. 2:7).

When God created Adam and Eve, He said, "Let Us make man in Our image, according to Our likeness" (Gen. 1:26a). Adam and Eve were each created with an identity in their inner being which was a direct reflection of God (Gen. 1:27; 2:21-22). "Our image," therefore, refers to identity. "Our likeness," on the other hand, refers to behavior. Adam and Eve were able to behave like God because they possessed His image. They were thus identified as children of God (Luke 3:38) and, as such, they behaved like God.

> "Then God said, 'Let Us make man in Our image, according to Our likeness.'"
> - Genesis 1:26a

THE INNER BEING OF HUMANS INCLUDES A SPIRIT

"the LORD . . . forms the spirit of man within him,"
- Zechariah 12:1b

God made Adam and Eve in His image as living beings (Gen. 1:26a), who each have a spirit which is limited (as opposed to God's infinite Spirit). It was necessary for God to create a spirit in human beings (Zech. 12:1b; Rom. 8:16; 1 Cor. 6:17) in order for them to have an intimate relationship with God, who is spirit (John 4:24).

...WITH SPIRITUAL SENSES

We know that God can see, hear, touch, taste, and smell but with spiritual, not physical, senses (Gen. 8:21; Job 1:11; 1 Pet. 3:2; Rev. 3:16). God also created humanity with spiritual senses to interact with Him. Because God is spirit, He relates to us through our spirit (1 Cor. 2:10-13). We can hear His inaudible voice in our minds (Matt. 10:19-20; 11:15), see Him through the spiritual eyes of faith (Eph. 1:18; Heb. 12:2), taste and smell His goodness in our spirit (Ps. 34:8), and touch and feel Him by faith.

...DESIGNED TO WORK IN AND WITH GOD'S SPIRIT

God designed mankind to express His nature (2 Cor. 4:7; 1 John 4:9). He empowered Adam and Eve to do this by placing His Spirit inside them. God designed a wonderfully intricate clay mold, then filled and animated it with His breath or Spirit. With His life inside them, they could relate to God through the Holy Spirit and enjoy eternal life (Gen. 2:7).

THE INNER BEING OF HUMANS INCLUDES A SOUL

"But we have this treasure in earthen vessels, that the surpassing greatness of the power may be of God and not from ourselves;"
- 2 Corinthians 4:7

Our soul is different from our spirit (1 Thess. 5:23; Heb. 4:12) and includes our mind, will, and emotions. With our mind, we think and process thoughts. With our will, we make decisions. With our emotions, we feel.

Though the soul is immaterial (not physical), other people can experience our soul through interactions in relationships. Another name for soul is personality. God designed humans to be expressive creatures. Each soul uniquely expresses its spiritual identity through the body (Rom. 12:1; 1 Cor. 12:18-20). A soul connected to God's life is a living soul.

HUMANS LIVE IN BODIES

Our physical bodies are the containers in which we live on this earth (2 Cor. 5:4; 2 Pet. 1:13). Our body is the instrument we use to interact with the physical world. God gave us five physical senses (seeing, hearing, touching, smelling, and tasting) to interact with other people and our physical environment. We have been uniquely designed to manifest God's glory in the physical world and rule over the earth as stewards under God's authority (Gen. 1:26; Ps. 8:4-8).

ILLUSTRATION: HUMANITY'S UNIQUE DESIGN

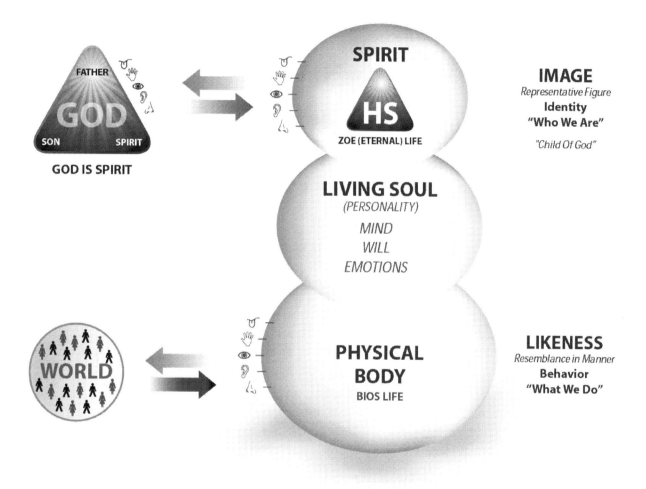

SUMMARY

Adam and Eve were made in the image of God, thus their core identity was "child of God." God uniquely designed humans as living beings who are each a spirit and soul (in His image), dwelling in a physical body and expressing themselves through their soul (with thoughts, emotions, and choices) and body (according to His likeness). As a result of this design, Adam and Eve enjoyed a personal relationship and intimate fellowship with God.

☩ TRANSFORM

1. What does it mean to me that I contain God's life?

   _____

   _____

   _____

   _____

   _____

2. What importance, or value, do I place on my spirit?

   _____

   _____

   _____

   _____

   _____

3. What might keep me from acknowledging this part of me?

   _____

   _____

   _____

   _____

   _____

4. If I have spiritual ears, in what ways do I hear God speak to me?

   _____

   _____

   _____

   _____

   _____

5. When God speaks to me, what emotions do I feel? What thoughts enter my mind? What decisions do I make in response?

_____

_____

_____

_____

_____

_____

6. Take some time to listen. What is the Holy Spirit telling me in this session?

_____

_____

_____

_____

_____

_____

_____

_____

_____

 **PRAY**

Father, thank You for making me special and distinct from everyone else in creation. "When I consider Your heavens, the work of Your fingers, the moon and the stars, which You have ordained; what is man that You take thought of him, and the son of man that You care for him? Yet You have made him a little lower than God, and You crown him with glory and majesty!" (Ps. 8:3-5) Thank You for designing me to enjoy a relationship with YOU! Thank You for giving me Your life to know, to experience, and to express. Amen

NEEDS OF HUMANITY
Supplied Life

CONNECT

- What has God revealed to you since we last met?

- What does the phrase "Supplied Life" mean to you? Who or what is the supplier?

- What makes you feel alive? What is satisfied in you that generates those feelings?

RENEW

GOD CREATED ADAM (MAN) WITH NEEDS

God created Adam with needs only He could meet. His design was to establish a relationship characterized by Adam's dependency, trust, surrender, intimacy, and obedience.

WHAT IS A NEED?

A need is something that MUST be met in order to live. Our physical needs consist of air, water, food, and rest. Without them we would physically die. Humans also have inner needs (Matt. 4:4; John 4:31-32).

WHAT ARE THOSE INNER NEEDS?

We gain some insight into our inner needs from Ephesians 5:33. In this verse, we see that a man needs respect and a woman needs love. Man's inner needs include respect, love

"...man does not live by bread alone, but man lives by everything that proceeds out of the mouth of the LORD." - Deuteronomy 8:3

(unconditional), acceptance (Rom. 15:7), significance ("I matter."), competency ("I am good at something."), etc. All these needs can be summarized in the need for worth or value. The inner needs of women will be discussed later in this session.

WHO IS SUPPOSED TO MEET HUMANITY'S NEEDS?

"And my God shall supply all your needs according to His riches in glory in Christ Jesus." - Philippians 4:19

God is our provider (Ps. 23:1; John 6:35; Acts 17:25; 2 Cor. 9:8; Phil. 4:19). Only God is qualified to meet our needs effectively. Because God is all-knowing, He is constantly aware of our needs (Matt. 6:8, 31-32; 10:29-30). Because God is all-powerful, He has the ability and resources to meet our needs (Ps. 145:15-16). Because God is all-present, He is continually with us, ready to meet our needs (Ps. 139:7-8).

WHAT IS THE DIFFERENCE BETWEEN NEED AND DESIRE?

People often confuse a desire with a need. As previously explained, an inner need (love, acceptance, worth, etc.) is something that MUST be met to live as God designed. A desire, however, is the yearning for something (i.e. love, acceptance, worth, accomplishment, pleasure, etc.). A need is always desired, but a desire is not always a need. Jesus expressed the difference when He told His disciples He desired to share the Last Supper with them (Luke 22:14-15). Jesus later told them they would scatter and leave Him alone, yet He was NOT alone because the Father was with Him, meeting His need for companionship (John 16:32). Jesus desired companionship with His friends but did not place any expectations on them to meet His needs.

WHY DID GOD CREATE ADAM TO HAVE NEEDS THAT ONLY GOD CAN MEET?

John 17 records a beautiful, intimate prayer between Jesus and the Father. In His prayer, Jesus acknowledges the love relationship that exists in the Trinity and how Jesus desires that believers enjoy that intimate relationship with God.

God designed Adam (humanity) in this way to establish a relationship characterized by God's provision and Adam's dependency (Gen. 1:29-30; 2:8-9, 16). This design allowed God to demonstrate WHO He is and allowed Adam to know Him better. It also allowed Adam to develop trust, surrender, and receptivity, which enhanced his intimacy with God. As God supplied ALL his needs, Adam felt worthwhile, fully valued, and completely alive.

GOD FASHIONED EVE (WOMAN)

God exists in relationship (Session 1) and created us to live in relationship (Matt. 22:37-39; John 17:24). He fashioned Eve to live in intimate relationship with Adam (Gen. 2:18-25) and to work with God to produce more life on earth (Gen. 1:28).

[?] At that point, what did Adam need from Eve? The answer was "nothing." He needed nothing from her because God alone was meeting his needs.

EVE (WOMAN) WAS CREATED WITH WHAT INNER NEEDS?

Eve (woman) needed the gentle kindness and considerateness of love. John 4:7–18 provides more insight. When Jesus encountered the woman at the well, He uncovered her deep, unmet need for acceptance and love as a result of her failed relationships. Eve's (or woman's) needs also included respect, acceptance, significance ("Do I contribute?"), competency ("Am I a good wife/friend/mother/employee?"). Again, as with Adam, these needs can be summed up in the need for worth or value.

[?] What then did Eve need from Adam? The answer again was "nothing" since God alone was meeting her needs.

"Jesus answered and said to her, 'Everyone who drinks of this water will thirst again; but whoever drinks of the water that I will give him shall never thirst; but the water that I will give him will become in him a well of water springing up to eternal life.'"
- John 4:13- 14

ILLUSTRATION: MEN AND WOMEN CREATED WITH NEEDS

NEEDS   NOTHING   **NEEDS**

 DESIRES

GIFT

 DESIRES

RESPECT	LOVE
LOVE	RESPECT
ACCEPTANCE	CONNECTEDNESS
ADEQUACY	THOUGHTFULNESS
ACHIEVEMENT	KINDNESS
ETC...	ETC...

FEELS WORTHWHILE WHEN NEEDS ARE MET   **FEELS WORTHWHILE WHEN NEEDS ARE MET**

"We love, because He first
loved us." - 1 John 4:19

ADAM AND EVE WERE FREE TO GIFT DESIRES TO EACH OTHER

As containers of God's life, Adam and Eve were filled to overflowing which resulted in them becoming expressers of God's life (John 7:37–39). With their needs met by God, they could then unconditionally gift to each other their desires (1 John 4:19).

SUMMARY

God designed humanity with needs only He can meet. This design established an intimate relationship characterized and enhanced by man's dependence on God's provision. Adam and Eve lived in a healthy relationship with God (loving Him), with themselves (loving themselves), and each other (based on unconditional love and enjoyment of His overflow to each other).

TRANSFORM

1. On what have I based my ultimate worth and value? (performance, appearance, intelligence, possessions, career, status, other's approval, etc.)

    _____

    _____

    _____

    _____

    _____

    _____

2. What are my needs? Which needs are most important to me?

    _____

    _____

    _____

    _____

    _____

    _____

3. Which attributes of God correspond to His ability to meet each need listed above?

_____

_____

_____

_____

_____

_____

_____

_____

4. In what ways have I seen God provide for my needs in the past?

_____

_____

_____

_____

_____

_____

_____

_____

 **PRAY**

Father, thank You for creating me with inner heart-needs which only You can meet. You alone are able to accurately and overwhelmingly tell me how much You love me unconditionally, how much You respect me, accept me, value my significance and competency which You have given me. You alone are the measure of my worth, based on Your delight in me. I believe this now and depend on You to meet my needs as the Source of my life. Now that my worth is determined by Your opinion of me, thank You for leading me into healthy relationships with myself and others. Amen.

PURPOSE OF HUMANITY
Expressed Life

 CONNECT

- What has God revealed to you since we last met?

- Name some examples of things built for a purpose where the design and function clearly express that purpose. (Example: a bridge)

- What was God's purpose in creating humanity?

- What is God's purpose for your life?

- In what ways are you fulfilling your purpose?

 RENEW

GOD CREATED HUMANITY FOR HIS GLORY

The prophet Isaiah tells us that God made humans for His glory (Is. 43:7). The Apostle Paul tells us that everything we do should be for God's glory (1 Cor. 10:31). Therefore, God created us to express or radiate His glory (Rev. 4:11; 21:9-11).

WHAT IS GLORY?

Glory is the visible expression or radiance of the beauty and character of God. In Exodus chapters 33 and 34, Moses asked to see God's glory. God responded by passing His goodness before him and telling Moses of His character.

The glory of God is beautiful and awe-inspiring (Ex. 34:5-7; Ps. 104:1).

> "Everyone who is called by My name, and whom I have created for My glory, whom I have formed, even whom I have made." - Isaiah 43:7

HOW DID ADAM AND EVE GLORIFY GOD?

God designed everything to express different aspects of His beauty and character (Ps. 19:1; Is. 6:3; Rom. 1:20). However, Adam and Eve were unique in their identity because they were made in God's image with the ability to express or glorify God in all their behavior. As the pinnacle of creation, they received a will separate from God's and were invited to rely solely on Him to meet their needs (Josh. 24:15). Within the intimate relationship Adam and Eve enjoyed with God, they were asked to continually yield to God's will (Gen. 2:15-17; Matt. 6:10). By choosing to trust God, depend on His resources, and operate under His direction, Adam and Eve manifested God's character, will, and life (glory) to each other (Gen. 1:28). This design is the same for all humanity (1 John 4:7).

WHAT ARE THE MECHANICS OF GLORIFYING GOD?

In Romans 7:22-23, Paul calls the process by which we manifest God's glory, the law, or principle of the mind. The principle works this way: God placed thoughts into Adam and Eve's minds regarding their character and daily activities; they processed those thoughts by searching their memories and emotions (Until the Fall, every interaction with God produced a good memory.); then they willingly chose to rely on God and obey His directions. Through this God-directed, God-empowered behavior, their purpose of sharing and expressing God's life was accomplished (1 Pet. 4:11). Before the Fall, they operated according to this principle of the mind moment by moment as they walked in intimate fellowship with God.

God supplied both the resources and the direction through the Holy Spirit within Adam. We see an example of this in Genesis 2:19. When he rested in God's provision and moved out under God's direction, Adam was living from the inside out much like a clay pot which contains and displays a treasure or a clay lamp which contains the oil that burns and produces light (Ps. 36:9; Matt. 5:14-16; 2 Cor. 4:7).

GLORIFYING GOD THROUGH LOVING RELATIONSHIPS

God's love is not a feeling, but rather a choice (Session 1). Choosing to live from God's resources and then following His lead describes how Adam loved God (John 15:5). What is the greatest commandment? A lawyer once asked Jesus what God wanted most from humanity. Jesus responded that God wanted people to love Him with all their heart, soul, and mind, and to love other people as they loved themselves (Matt. 22:35-39; 1 John 3:23).

Because we know God is love (1 John 4:8), we understand Jesus was simply saying God wants us to contain His life (which is love), then share it back with Him, with ourselves, and with others (Rom. 5:5; 1 John 3:11, 23; 4:9, 19). When we display the love of God, we are expressing or glorifying God (John 13:35). Each time we receive from God and give to God and others, we complete a healthy relationship cycle.

When thinking about the purpose of man, it is helpful to think of a light bulb. Essentially glass and metal, a light bulb has been formed in such a way that when it is connected to a power source, it will project light. In order to fulfill its purpose, the bulb must be both functional (not broken) and connected to an energy source.

ILLUSTRATION: THE MECHANICS OF GLORIFYING GOD

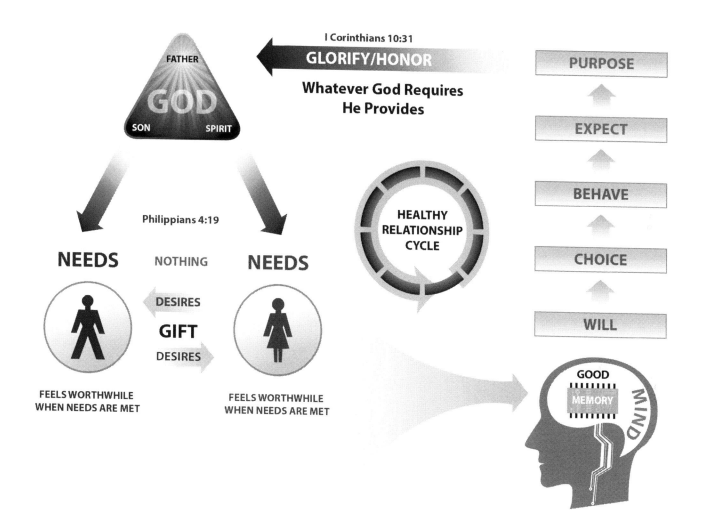

SUMMARY

God created man and woman to enjoy intimate fellowship with Him and to display His life (glorify God). Paul described the mechanics of glorifying God as the principle of the mind: 1) we receive a thought from the Spirit, 2) we process that thought, 3) we choose to submit our will to His direction, and 4) we carry out that action empowered by the Spirit. This process describes how to love God and, in turn, love ourselves and others. When we rest in God's provision and move only under His direction, we live from the inside out, accomplishing God's purpose for humanity.

TRANSFORM

1. In what ways have I seen creation glorify God?

   _____

   _____

   _____

   _____

   _____

2. How has the glory of God, as seen in creation, impacted my life?

   _____

   _____

   _____

   _____

   _____

3. In what ways have I seen the glory of God in another person?

   _____

   _____

   _____

   _____

   _____

4. In what ways have I expressed the glory of God? What did it look like? What did it feel like?

   _____

   _____

   _____

   _____

   _____

5. What will indicate to me and others that I am truly expressing God's life and nature?

_____

_____

_____

_____

6. Take some time to listen. What is the Holy Spirit telling me in this session?

_____

_____

_____

_____

7. How will the Holy Spirit's revelation impact my beliefs, choices, and behaviors?

_____

_____

_____

_____

_____

 **PRAY**

Father, You are beautiful in every way. Your character is beyond reproach. Your power is matchless. You are amazing. Thank You for creating me and giving me purpose in living. Thank You that I get to live by Your provision and display Your beauty, character, and power through my fragile body. May I mentally choose to rest in Your provision for me today and then radiate Your glorious life and love to others so that they may see my good deeds and glorify You. Amen.

THE TWO TREES
Life and Death

5

CONNECT

- What has God revealed to you since we last met?

- How did God intend for Adam and Eve to realize a life of meaning, purpose, and fulfillment?

- What other option was available to Adam and Eve?

- When there are choices to be made, how do you decide what to do?

- What is the purpose of the tree of life and the tree of the knowledge of good and evil in the garden of Eden?

RENEW

THE TWO TREES

The historical account of the two trees begins when God created a paradise on the earth known as the Garden of Eden. The garden contained a variety of fruit bearing trees, two of which He placed in the center of the garden, the tree of life and the tree of the knowledge of good and evil. Adam and Eve were given the option to eat freely from the variety of fruit bearing trees with the exception of one, the tree of the knowledge of good and evil (Gen. 2:16-17).

LOVE IS A CHOICE

One of God's greatest gifts to Adam and Eve was this freedom to make choices. The ability to choose allowed them to love like God. As we discussed in Session 1, God's love

> "Out of the ground the LORD God caused to grow every tree that is pleasing to the sight and good for food; the tree of life also in the midst of the garden, and the tree of the knowledge of good and evil."
>
> - Genesis 2:9

"In God there is no hunger that needs to be filled, only plenteousness that desires to give." - C.S. Lewis

is not a feeling but a choice which displays a commitment. This love is a conscious, free will decision to unconditionally act in the best interest of another (John 14:23; 15:13; 1 Cor. 13:4-7).

Adam and Eve outwardly expressed their love for God by choosing to trust in Him and remain faithful to His word. Every time Adam and Eve refrained from eating from the tree of the knowledge of good and evil, their love for God was displayed (John 14:15).

This love was the driving motivation which sustained Adam and Eve's relationship with God. Their love was rooted in the truth that the Creator always fulfilled His word and acted in their best interest (Deut. 7:9; Ps. 116:5; John 17:17).

Knowing the truth has huge implications in our life. For most of recorded history, people had no idea germs existed because germs are not visible without a microscope. People acted as if they did not exist. Doctors did not wash their hands before medical procedures. Without the truth, many people died from the resulting infections.

A CHOICE BETWEEN TWO DISTINCT SYSTEMS

Every time Adam and Eve walked past those two trees in the middle of the garden they faced a choice. They could eat from the tree of life, or they could eat from the tree of the knowledge of good and evil. The two paths were opposed to each other and were distinguished by conflicting characteristics (Matt. 7:13-14). Let's look at some of the aspects that define these distinctly different systems for living.

TRUTH VS. THE LIE

The tree of life symbolizes the truth or reality about life and our design. God's words are truth (Ps. 119:160; John 17:17), and when we choose to believe His words, we can walk in truth (Matt. 4:4; 2 Pet. 1:12; 3 John 1:4).

The tree of the knowledge of good and evil represents the lie of self-sufficiency (Rom. 1:25). We break from reality when we imagine meeting our own needs apart from the God who made all things and holds all things together (Col. 1:16-17; Heb. 1:3).

RECEIVING VS. ACHIEVING

The tree of life represents a system where we receive from the hand of God everything required to experience a life of meaning, purpose, and fulfillment (1 Chr. 29:12; 1 Cor. 4:7; 2 Cor. 3:5). When we rest in God's provision, we bring glory and honor to God (Phil. 4:13, 19; 2 Pet. 1:3; Rev. 4:11). In this system, humanity walks in trust and dependence on God (Ps. 62:5).

The tree of the knowledge of good and evil represents a system where one must achieve or earn glory and honor for one's self (Prov. 25:27b). Instead of receiving from God, Adam could freely choose to act on what he believed best enabled him to meet his own needs (Gen. 3:4-5). In this system, humanity strives to walk in prideful independence from God (1 John 2:16).

GOD'S WISDOM VS. SELF-REASONING

Wisdom is the knowledge and discernment needed to make decisions leading to the best outcomes. As humans, we are not born with wisdom, but we are in desperate need of it (Prov. 3:13-18). We must acquire it along the way (Prov. 4:7).

The tree of life symbolizes the wisdom of God. Because God exists in the past, present, and future simultaneously (John 8:58), He possesses all wisdom and understanding (Job 12:13). God offers wisdom freely to those who choose to come to Him and ask (James 1:5).

The tree of the knowledge of good and evil represents self-reasoning. Without God, who possesses all wisdom, we are left to our own reasoning. The Bible says man's reasoning is foolishness (1 Cor. 1:20; 3:19). Without God's wisdom, we stumble around speculating about what is right and wrong and what will meet our needs (Rom. 1:21). God calls this doing whatever is right in one's own eyes (Judg. 17:6).

> "But if any of you lacks wisdom, let him ask of God, who gives to all men generously and without reproach, and it will be given to him."
> - James 1:5

TRUST AND PEACE VS. DOUBT AND FEAR

The tree of life represents a choice to trust in God. Once on the path of trusting God, we are surrounded by His peace (Is. 26:3). Placing our faith and trust in God leads us to inner peace (Rom. 15:13). Knowing and believing God will take care of our needs (Phil. 4:19) and will always be with us (Matt. 28:20; Heb. 13:5-6) allows us to experience the peace that passes all understanding (Phil. 4:7).

The tree of the knowledge of good and evil represents doubt (Gen. 3:1-5). When we doubt the goodness and provision of God, the only person left on whom we can rely is our self (Ps. 146:3). The Bible calls this idolatry (1 Sam. 15:22-23; Jer. 2:13). Those who entertain doubt about God and have a false concept of God often struggle with overwhelming feelings of fear, anxiety, insecurity, and inadequacy (Matt. 14:28-32).

> "Now may the God of hope fill you with all joy and peace in believing, that you may abound in hope by the power of the Holy Spirit."
> - Romans 15:13

FREEDOM VS. BONDAGE

The tree of life represents freedom. God's freedom is not the ability to gratify evil desires, rather it is freedom from the power of sin and freedom to be who God designed us to be – containers of His life and love (Rom. 8:2). To live in any other way than what God purposed is bondage.

The tree of the knowledge of good and evil represents bondage. Because sin is a self-centered choice, it binds our heart to a counterfeit existence. Jesus said that anyone who sins is a slave to sin (John 8:34).

> "For the law of the Spirit of life in Christ Jesus has set you free from the law of sin and of death." - Romans 8:2

LIFE VS. DEATH

The tree of life represents God's life, one without beginning or end (Session 1) (Ps. 90:2; John 1:1-4; Rev. 21:6). A person enters God's life through an intimate relationship with

"This is eternal life, that they may know You, the only true God, and Jesus Christ whom You have sent."

- John 17:3

the Person who is life (John 14:6; 17:3). Eating from a fruit tree illustrates this truth. Just as fruit supplies sustenance and strength to our body, so too the Holy Spirit in our spirit sustains, strengthens, empowers, and animates us with His life (John 6:56, 63; Acts 1:8; 2 Tim. 1:7).

The tree of the knowledge of good and evil represents death. God told Adam if he chose to eat of this tree, he would die (Gen. 2:17). Death is the absence of life. If we reject God's way of life, the only other system is death (Prov. 14:12). Although the fruit from this tree looks good for food, it offers no sustenance for life and results in death (Eccl. 2:22-23).

ILLUSTRATION: THE TWO TREES IN THE GARDEN

"The LORD God commanded the man, saying, 'From any tree of the garden you may eat freely; but from the tree of the knowledge of good and evil you shall not eat, for in the day that you eat from it you will surely die.'"

- Genesis 2:16, 17

Life

Knowledge of Good and Evil

THE TRUTH
RECEIVING SYSTEM
GOD'S WISDOM
TRUST AND PEACE
FREEDOM
LIFE

THE LIE
ACHIEVING SYSTEM
SELF-REASONING
DOUBT AND FEAR
BONDAGE
DEATH

SUMMARY

The two trees in the middle of the Garden of Eden represent a choice between two systems for living. The tree of life represents an option to trust God which leads to meaning, purpose, and fulfillment. The tree of the knowledge of good and evil represents an option to rely on perception, experience, and self-reasoning apart from God, resulting in death.

TRANSFORM

1. What does a life of meaning, purpose, and fulfillment look like to me?

    _____

    _____

    _____

    _____

2. Which characteristic of the Tree of Life encourages me most? Why?

    _____

    _____

    _____

    _____

3. When faced with a problem, from which tree/system do I tend to operate? Why is that?

    _____

    _____

    _____

    _____

4. In what ways have I operated from the tree of the knowledge of good and evil? What were the results?

    _____

    _____

    _____

    _____

5. When in my life have I been fearful? What role did doubt play in that fear?

    _____

    _____

    _____

    _____

6. Take some time to listen. What is the Holy Spirit telling me in this session?

_____

_____

_____

_____

_____

7. How will the Holy Spirit's revelation impact my beliefs, choices, and behaviors?

_____

_____

_____

_____

_____

_____

 **PRAY**

Father, enlighten the eyes of my heart so that I may walk in Your paths. Your word is a light to my path and a lamp to my feet. Lord, I trust that You have my best interest at heart all the time regardless of what my eyes tell me. Bring me to the place where I can truly live and experience the life in which You have uniquely fashioned and equipped me to walk. I now realize that any other way will ultimately lead to frustration and futility. I recognize how making choices based solely on my perceptions can lead to misery and heartache. Lord, this day I place my confidence solely in Your word. Day by day and moment-by-moment I wish to lead the life You have purposed for me - to be an expression of Your life, to glorify You. Today I choose freedom over bondage and life over death. Thank You for sending Jesus, Your Living Word, to redeem me from the empty way of life I once lived by doing what was right in my own eyes. Amen.

CONSEQUENCES OF THE FALL
Loss of Life

6

 CONNECT

- What has God revealed to you since we last met?

- What is the difference between life and death?

- What does it mean to be separated from God?

- What happened to humanity when Adam and Eve chose to eat from the tree of the knowledge of good and evil?

 RENEW

THE FALL OF HUMANITY

In Genesis 3:1-5, we read where Satan appeared to Eve as a serpent. He questioned her understanding of the commandment God gave to Adam, "Indeed, has God said, 'You shall not eat from any tree of the garden'?" (Gen. 3:1). Through this question he paved the way to deceive Eve. His goal was simply to lead Adam and Eve to disobey God by eating a piece of fruit (2 Cor. 11:3).

After Eve repeated God's commandment to Satan, he placed a temptation in her mind. Satan said to her, "You surely will not die! For God knows that in the day you eat from it your eyes will be opened, and you will be like God, knowing good and evil" (Gen. 3:4-5). In this temptation he mixed truth with a lie. It was true that their eyes would be opened, and they would know good and evil. However, the big lie was, "You surely will not die!"

Satan hooked Eve through the statement "you will be like God." The truth was they were already like God. God had placed His life in them, which they expressed through their

> "The serpent said to the woman, 'You surely will not die! For God knows that in the day you eat from it your eyes will be opened, and you will be like God, knowing good and evil.'"
> - Genesis 3:4-5

behavior. Satan's deception appealed to every aspect of her design. Eve ate the fruit when she "saw that the tree was good for food, and that it was a delight to the eyes, and that the tree was desirable to make one wise" (Gen. 3:6). The truth was they already had an abundance of food, beauty, and wisdom. After all, God met all their needs through His life.

Once Eve bought into the lie and believed it was what she wanted (free will), she ate the fruit and gave it to Adam, and he ate (Gen. 3:6). Now we will look at the consequences of their choice.

LIFE LEFT ADAM AND EVE – HUMANITY DIED

God told Adam that on the day he ate from the tree of the knowledge of good and evil, he would "surely die" (Gen. 2:16 -17). You may have noticed no funeral is mentioned in Genesis 3; the physical bodies of Adam and Eve continued to function. So, in what way did they die? Remember, they were created spiritual beings as well as physical. Adam and Eve still had a spirit, but without God's life they were now spiritually dead because death is the absence of life. After the Holy Spirit left, they no longer contained God's life (John 6:63; 1 John 5:12). God's life can be described as eternal love, joy, peace, fulfillment, purpose, enjoyment, value, meaning, completion, abundance, rest, fullness, and satisfaction. Spiritual death is the absence of these qualities.

ADAM AND EVE WERE SEPARATED FROM GOD

Did God separate Himself from Adam and Eve when they sinned? Absolutely not! God went looking for them in their fallen state (Gen. 3:9). God did not change (Mal. 3:6); Adam and Eve changed. They separated themselves from God (Is. 53:6a; 59:2).

This separation resulted in a transfer from light to darkness; life to death; full to empty; freedom to bondage; love to hate. Their perception changed forever. They did not lose their memories of the garden or of their relationship with God, but their perception of those memories was twisted and no longer understood through God's life (Rom. 1:20-22).

> "And you were dead in your trespasses and sins, in which you formerly walked according to the course of this world, according to the prince of the power of the air, of the spirit that is now working in the sons of disobedience. Among them we too all formerly lived in the lusts of our flesh, indulging the desires of the flesh and of the mind, and were by nature children of wrath, even as the rest."
> - Ephesians 2:1-3

Death is the absence of life just like darkness is the absence of light. When Adam and Eve rebelled against life Himself, they cut themselves off from containing the life and light of God.

IDENTITY CHANGED

Were Adam and Eve still considered children of God? Without God's life (Holy Spirit), they lost their original identity. Fathered in nature by Satan, they became children of the devil (John 8:44; Rom. 5:19; Eph. 2:1-3; 1 John 3:10). Now they were sinners with a sin nature. Paul refers to the sinner as the "old self" in Romans 6:6.

While spiritually alive, godliness and righteousness characterized their behaviors. After the Fall, sinning became their natural action.

"For as through the one man's disobedience the many were made sinners..."
- Romans 5:19a

SOUL MERELY EXISTED

Adam and Eve did not lose their souls. However, cut off from God's life, they changed from living souls to souls who merely existed. Instead of expressing God's life, their souls expressed their sinful nature through their thoughts, emotions, and choices.

NEEDS NO LONGER MET

Did God stop meeting Adam and Eve's needs? After the Fall, God prohibited them from living in the garden, but He graciously clothed them with animal skins (Gen. 3:21). He provided property to cultivate food (Gen. 3:23) and continued to communicate with them (Gen. 4:6-7). However, because they were spiritually dead, they were unable to receive God's life.

They continually tried to meet their needs through human power and physical resources. Instead of living from the inside out (depending on God to meet their needs), they now lived from the outside in. Sadly, they were empty vessels unable to produce life for themselves. Without God's life, their deepest needs went unmet (Jer. 2:13; 17:5-6).

"Thus says the LORD, 'Cursed is the man who trusts in mankind and makes flesh his strength, and whose heart turns away from the LORD. For he will be like a bush in the desert and will not see when prosperity comes, But will live in stony wastes in the wilderness, a land of salt without inhabitant.'"
- Jeremiah 17:5-6

LAW (PRINCIPLE) OF SIN ENTERED

When Adam and Eve ate the forbidden fruit, they sinned. Sin can be described as "missing the mark." Before their fall, Adam and Eve always hit the "mark" of holiness and righteousness because they operated from God's life. Now as a result of their spiritual death, indwelling sin entered their physical bodies.

Paul referred to this indwelling sin (Rom. 7:17, 20) as the "law of sin" in Romans 7:23. Indwelling sin can be compared to gravity. Just as gravity pulls our physical bodies downward, so also indwelling sin pulls us downward to gratify the desires of the flesh.

BODIES BEGAN TO DECAY

Before the Fall, Adam and Eve were designed to live eternally. As a result of the Fall, the physical world was infected with sin. The human body became subject to the contamination of sin, the process of decay, and death (Gen. 3:19; Eccl. 12:7; 2 Cor. 5:1-4).

"By the sweat of your face you will eat bread, till you return to the ground..."
- Genesis 3:19a

PROGRAMMED FLESH DEVELOPED

When Adam and Eve were alive, they did not need to do anything to meet their own needs. They did not need to protect or defend themselves; God established and protected them (Ps. 36:7-10).

After Adam and Eve lost life, they developed coping mechanisms to meet their needs (Eccl. 7:29). The first thing they felt was shame from their nakedness, so they covered themselves. Then hearing God walking in the garden, they hid in fear because of their guilt. Finally, confronted with their sin, they blamed someone else. Eve blamed the serpent. Adam blamed Eve and God. Their initial coping mechanisms were covering, hiding, and blaming (Gen. 3:7-13).

In his letters, the Apostle Paul refers to these coping mechanisms which turn into habit patterns as "the flesh" (Rom. 7:18; 8:3-8).

ILLUSTRATION: HUMANITY AFTER THE FALL

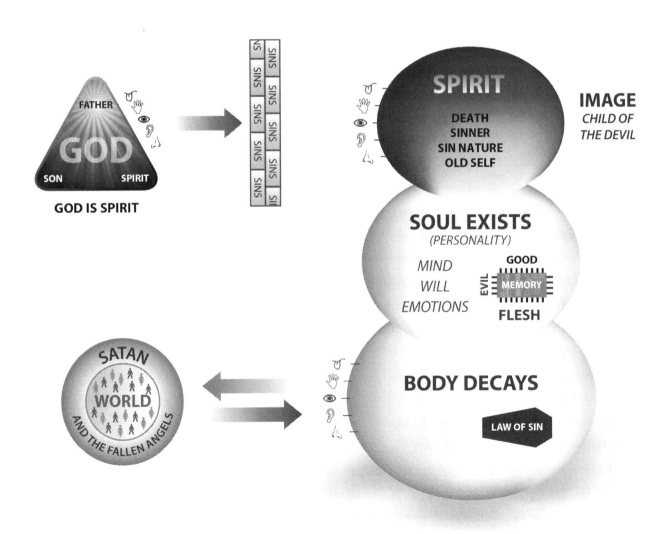

CONDEMNED

Removed from the garden (Gen. 3:24), Adam and Eve could no longer experience the life they had formerly known. They stood condemned, living under judgment from the guilt of sinning against God (Rom. 5:16a).

"...judgment arose from one transgression resulting in condemnation..."
- Romans 5:16a

ALL HUMANITY AFFECTED

Because the entire human race descended from Adam and Eve, the Bible teaches that humanity was in Adam and Eve when they sinned against God. As a result:

- When Adam died spiritually, all of humanity died spiritually (1 Cor. 15:22a).

- When Adam became a sinner, all of humanity became sinners (Rom. 5:19a).

- When Adam's needs went unmet, all of humanity's needs went unmet (Jer. 2:13).

- When Adam was condemned, all of humanity was condemned (Rom. 5:18a).

"For as through the one man's disobedience the many were made sinners,"
- Romans 5:19a

ILLUSTRATION: HUMANITY DIED IN ADAM

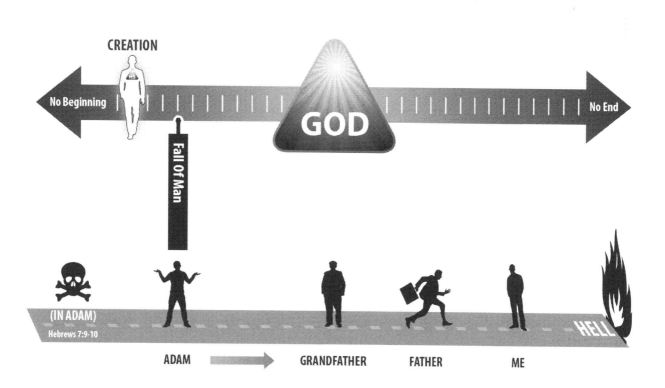

A BROKEN SYSTEM OF EXISTING EMERGES

"There is a way which seems right to a man, But its end is the way of death."
- Proverbs 14:12

The original system of life and freedom differed greatly from the broken system of existing after the Fall. The first system was generated by God's life in Adam and Eve. Every thought, feeling, and choice reflected God's life in them.

After the Fall, their broken system could be described as a system of choice. The knowledge of good and evil replaced God's life. The quality of their existence now depended on their choices. If they chose good, they might experience pleasure; if they chose evil, they would experience unpleasant consequences. Without God's life initiating their thoughts, emotions, and will, they depended on their flesh to navigate the choices before them (Judg. 17:6; Prov. 14:12).

This broken system produced laws, rules, guidelines, boundaries, principles, precepts, and, ultimately, religion to guide one toward hope for success. However, no life exists in this system (Col. 2:8, 20-23).

ILLUSTRATION: A BROKEN SYSTEM OF EXISTING

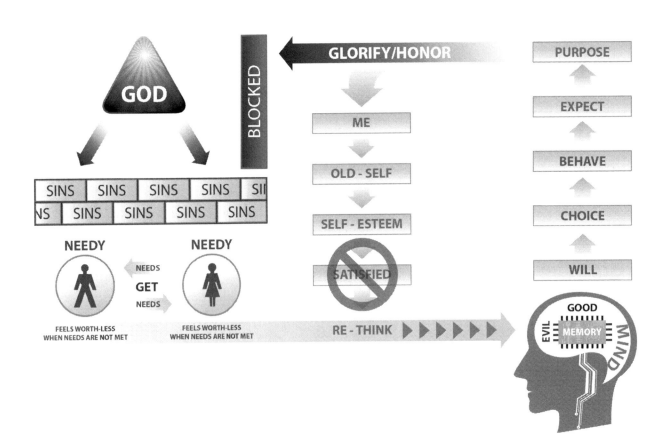

SUMMARY

As a consequence of the Fall, Adam and Eve lost God's life, resulting in spiritual death and separation from God. Their physical bodies began to decay. They began to look for sources other than God to meet their needs. Their spiritual death produced a sin nature that changed their identity from children of God to children of Satan. The law of sin entered their bodies, and they developed coping mechanisms to try to meet their needs in the flesh. Adam's and Eve's fallen (condemned) condition has been passed down to all humanity.

TRANSFORM

1. What was my life like before receiving God's salvation?

_____

_____

_____

_____

2. What are my thoughts when I feel dead or empty?

_____

_____

_____

_____

3. At what times in my life have I felt shame and condemnation?

_____

_____

_____

_____

4. How does knowing the consequences of the Fall change the way I see others who are not Christians?

_____

_____

_____

_____

5. Take some time to listen. What is the Holy Spirit telling me in this session?

_____

_____

_____

_____

_____

_____

_____

6. How will the Holy Spirit's revelation impact my beliefs, choices, and behaviors?

_____

_____

_____

_____

_____

_____

_____

 **PRAY**

Father, I acknowledge You as the giver of life. Apart from You, I cannot meet my own needs. I cannot control anyone or anything around me in order to experience freedom in this world. Thank You for the freedom You give through Your life-giving Spirit in me. Today, reveal the ways I may default to my flesh to meet my needs. Thank You Father that Your grace is sufficient and Your power is perfected in my weakness. Instead of being immobilized by having to make the right choice, I will trust in You and surrender to Your will. Amen.

DEVELOPMENT OF FLESH
Counterfeit Life

CONNECT

- What has God revealed to you since we last met?

- What kind of things do people do to meet their needs for worth, love, respect, and acceptance?

- What patterns or habits develop as people continue in these behaviors?

- What does counterfeit mean to you?

RENEW

WHAT IS FLESH?

When you hear the word flesh, what comes to mind? The word flesh can mean the meat of an animal. However, the apostle Paul, in many of his letters to churches in the New Testament, used it to represent something deeper. The word Paul used was the Greek word "sarx." It means "of the natural," "physically-driven," or "materialistic" (1 John 2:16). Defined this way, flesh is the material resource we use in an attempt to meet needs apart from God. Other terms for flesh are "coping mechanisms" or "making life work."

We are all created with inner needs for love, acceptance, and worth (to name a few) which only God can meet (Matt. 4:4; John 4:14; 6:35). Born without God (Eph. 2:1-3; 4:17-19), we try to meet these needs by physical resources and the people around us. Indeed, Satan deceived Eve by redirecting her thoughts from dependence on God toward a material object (fruit) to meet her needs (Gen. 3:4-6). Just as Adam and Eve ate from the tree of the knowledge of good and evil, so too their descendants continue to choose the same fleshly system of self-reasoning and achieving (Session 5).

σάρξ

Sarx is a Greek word frequently used in the New Testament. It is most literally translated "flesh."

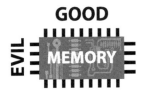

Just like a computer can be programmed to direct the response of a machine, so also, we can learn and carry out default (pro-grammed) ways to handle life out of our fleshly resources. In effect, we program ourselves.

PROGRAMMED FLESH

Have you ever heard someone say, "I just want to be happy"? What would it take to make you happy or satisfied? Without God, we seek happiness or satisfaction through self-rea-soning, trial and error, and gathering worldly wisdom from others (Prov. 14:12; 1 Cor. 3:19-20). Over time, our thinking and consequently our behaviors form patterns. People try to get their needs met in a wide variety of ways. Efforts which fail to produce the desired benefits are not repeated. Actions that achieve even the slightest need-meeting potential are repeated. Simply stated, people want to maximize pleasure and minimize pain. When fleshly behaviors are continually repeated, they become programmed into our memory and trigger default-responses (habits) (Rom. 7:18, 25; Gal. 5:16-21; Phil. 3:3-6). For instance, if wearing a certain outfit prompts a compliment, we tend to wear it again. Resorting to angry words to punish someone who insults us is another fleshly action. If demeaning the other person makes us feel better in the moment, we are more likely to try angry words the next time we are insulted. A third example of the flesh is controlling others or demanding their respect by physical domination. Again, if we feel some respect and power, we will probably continue to physically intimidate others. Ses-sion 15 lists more examples of manifestations of the flesh.

ILLUSTRATION: HOW FLESH IS PROGRAMMED

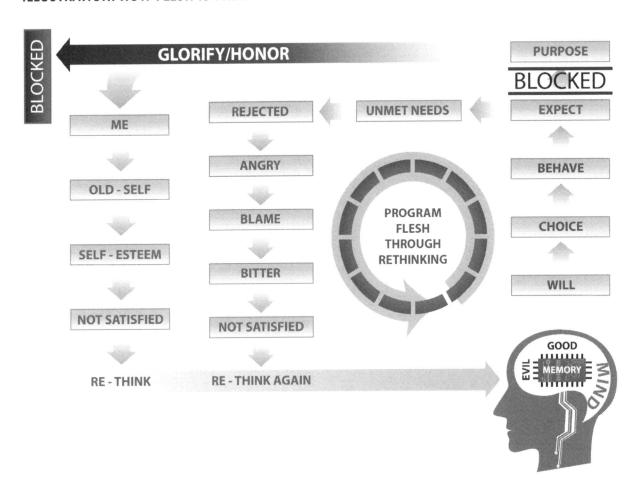

CAN OUR FLESH EVER FULLY MEET OUR INNER NEEDS?

Neither the material things of this world nor other people will ever fully satisfy our needs (Rom. 6:21). The pain of unmet needs results in conclusions about our failed attempts and beliefs about ourselves, leading to a new cycle of rethinking. Jeremiah 17:5-6 vividly describes the negative consequence of looking to the flesh to meet our needs when it declares, "Cursed is the man who trusts in mankind and makes flesh his strength, and whose heart turns away from the LORD. For he will be like a bush in the desert and will not see when prosperity comes, but will live in stony wastes in the wilderness, a land of salt without inhabitant."

FLESH IS A CONTROLLER

Flesh strives to control the environment to manufacture results which bring success, worth, and security. Flesh is also an attempt to establish an identity, by an action or an inaction, and to attain a desired life by controlling every possible outcome (Prov. 14:12).

FLESH IS INHERITED

1 Peter 1:18b says we inherited our futile way of life from our forefathers. What does that mean to you?

Because we are born "dead to God" (Eph. 2:1-3), we must learn how to get our needs met somewhere else. The first flesh patterns we learn usually come from family. We grow up observing our parents' way of operating in the flesh, and many times we adopt those measures for ourselves. Too often, as sons or daughters, we vow not to be like our parents only to find ourselves unconsciously imitating them.

One example of this pattern is the way Isaac learned from his father, Abraham, to lie for self-protection. This flesh pattern was continued and magnified to an even greater degree in the life of Isaac's son, Jacob.

The Bible is full of stories of people who relied on their flesh to try to meet their needs. One example is King Saul, who took it upon himself to offer sacrifices himself instead of waiting on Samuel as God had instructed. Saul was under stress because his army was deserting. Instead of looking to God in faith, he acted using his reasoning and his resources. The consequences for Saul were severe. This complete story is found in 1 Samuel 13:6-14.

ABRAHAM
Lied for self protection.
(Gen. 12:13; 20:2)

ISAAC
Lied for self protection.
(Gen. 26:7)

JACOB
Lied for personal gain.
(Gen. 27:18-19)

"If anyone else has a mind to put confidence in the flesh, I far more: circumcised the eighth day, of the nation of Israel, of the tribe of Benjamin, a Hebrew of Hebrews; as to the Law, a Pharisee; as to zeal, a persecutor of the church; as to the righteousness which is in the Law, found blameless."
- Philippians 3:4-6

CONFIDENCE BASED FLESH

Confidence based flesh is a dependence on self, characterized by confidence in one's own abilities. This type of flesh frequently develops when positive messages of love, acceptance, affirmation, praise, encouragement, and support are poured out repeatedly on a child. This belief is reinforced if that person achieves great success in their endeavors. An example of confident flesh is Paul's flesh as described in Philippians 3:3-6.

ILLUSTRATION: CONFIDENCE BASED FLESH

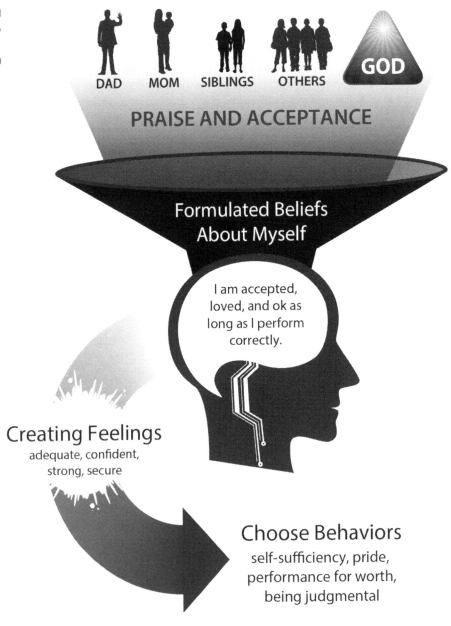

SHAME BASED FLESH

Shame based flesh is also a dependence on self, characterized by a low view of one's self. This type of flesh develops when negative feedback or messages are repeatedly delivered through rejection, shame, humiliation, accusation, abuse (verbal or otherwise), neglect, detachment, or absence. This belief system can be reinforced through failure to achieve. The person with shame based flesh might believe messages like "I am unloved, ugly, stupid, and defective" or "Something is wrong with me."

ILLUSTRATION: SHAME BASED FLESH

One example of shame based flesh is the woman at the well in John 4. Another person in the Bible who operated out of shame based flesh was King Saul's grandson Mephibosheth, who calls himself a "dead dog." - 2 Samuel 9:8

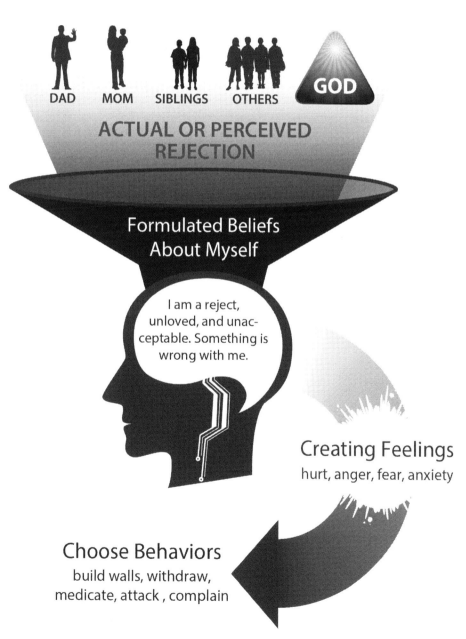

DAD   MOM   SIBLINGS   OTHERS   GOD

ACTUAL OR PERCEIVED REJECTION

Formulated Beliefs About Myself

I am a reject, unloved, and unacceptable. Something is wrong with me.

Creating Feelings
hurt, anger, fear, anxiety

Choose Behaviors
build walls, withdraw, medicate, attack , complain

FLESH IS UNIQUE TO EACH INDIVIDUAL

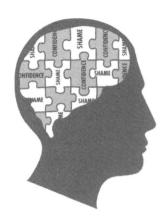

Confidence and shame based flesh are examples of two distinct paths of flesh development. These two extremes help us understand how messages received become formulated beliefs that lead to specific coping behaviors (belief drives behavior). Most of us, however, have a combination of confidence and shame based flesh. Each of us develops our own flesh patterns combining confidence and shame depending on the circumstances and messages we receive. Our parents may give us approval and affirmation, leading to confidence and self-reliance in certain abilities or attributes. On the other hand, our peers may tease or bully us, leading to shame and fear which can result in avoidance, hostility, or addictions. The actions we take can often look confident at face value, but may be done out of fear of failure or rejection (i.e. a person is driven to winning at all cost by the fear of failure). We may take actions that look shameful, but may be done out of self-confidence and disregard for others (i.e. a person commits adultery with another married person). The many ways in which our fleshly actions manifest themselves are infinite and unique to each of us.

SUMMARY

Born with a nature that is hostile toward God's love, acceptance, and value, everyone develops ways (flesh patterns) to make life work and meet their own needs apart from God. Whether confidence based or shame based, all flesh patterns result from false beliefs which lead to self-effort and futility.

TRANSFORM

1. In what ways do I see these behaviors called "flesh" in people around me?

    _____

    _____

    _____

    _____

2. What behaviors have I developed that came from frustration, anxiety, or discontent?

    _____

    _____

    _____

    _____

3. What events or messages have shaped my belief system?

    _____

    _____

    _____

4. Do I see myself exhibiting confidence based flesh, shame based flesh, or a combination of the two? What thoughts or behaviors demonstrate that in my life?

    _____

    _____

    _____

5. Take some time to listen. What is the Holy Spirit telling me in this session?

    _____

    _____

    _____

6. How will the Holy Spirit's revelation impact my beliefs, choices, and behaviors?

    _____

    _____

    _____

 **PRAY**

Father, lead me in this process of recognizing my flesh. Reveal to me the futile and even destructive results when I operate out of my own self-sufficiency. Remind me of Your sufficiency as You lead me on this journey of discovering lies about myself which have resulted in behaviors to protect or assert myself. Help me to understand others when they operate in the flesh, and enable me to see them through Your eyes. Thank You for this opportunity to know You better and for revealing anything in my life which hinders our relationship. Amen.

GOD'S SOLUTION AND OUR RESPONSE

Provision for Life

CONNECT

- What has God revealed to you since we last met?

- What are the barriers to beginning a close, personal relationship with God?

- In what ways have people tried to remove these barriers?

- Describe the Gospel of Jesus Christ in a few sentences.

- What justifies you before God?

RENEW

TWO PROBLEMS WITH HUMANITY AFTER THE FALL

Adam's sin brought about two problems for his descendants. These problems are barriers to the fulfillment of God's design and purpose for humanity.

PROBLEM #1: OUR SINS

Acts of rebellion against God, also known as sin, present a big problem for mankind (Rom. 3:23). Instead of displaying the love and life of God, humanity displays selfishness and evil (Eph. 4:17-19). Whether we feel guilty or not, our sin incites the wrath of a holy and just God Who declares us guilty (Rom. 1:18; Col. 3:6). Our rebellion makes us enemies of the very life we need (Rom. 5:10). We cannot fix this problem ourselves (Matt. 19:26). Indeed, because of our old self (see problem #2 below), we pile up more offenses resulting in more guilt and wrath (Rom. 2:5-6).

"for all have sinned and fall short of the glory of God,"
- Romans 3:23

PROBLEM #2: OUR OLD SELF

Every descendant of Adam is born into this world a lifeless sinner, also referred to in the New Testament as the "old self" or "old man" (Rom. 6:6; Eph. 2:1; 4:22; Col. 3:9). Along with a dead spirit, we inherited an identity as unrighteous beings, full of shame (Gen. 3:7-13; 1 Cor. 6:9a; 2 Pet. 2:12-15). Shame is both a condition and a consciousness that we are defective and unacceptable. After Adam's sin, humanity lost the ability to contain God's life. Just as a broken glass cannot hold water, that first sin damaged Adam, making it impossible for him to contain God's life (Jer. 17:9). The apostle Paul also described humanity in their fallen state as children of wrath who have a natural bent toward rebellion against God (Eph. 2:3). Our dead spirit cannot be reformed or fixed (Gal. 2:16). It is damaged beyond repair and must be replaced (John 3:3).

GOD'S SOLUTION TO OUR PROBLEMS

Even though we cannot fix our two problems, God had a plan from the beginning to solve them (Rom. 5:6; Eph. 1:4; Rev. 13:8). His plan involved the crucifixion of His Son, Jesus Christ. As a result of the cross of Christ, our two problems were dealt with and eradicated. Through the provision of Christ's death, God removed both the offenses AND the offender, saving us from our sins and our self. He forgave our sinful behavior (our guilt) and crucified our sinful nature (our shame).

FORGIVEN, CLEANSED, RECONCILED AND JUSTIFIED

God demonstrated His love for us through the sacrificial death of Christ (Rom. 5:8). Through the suffering of Christ, culminating in the shedding of His blood on the cross, He bore God's wrath toward sin (Is. 53:5-6; 1 John 2:2). Jesus, who never sinned, willingly bore our sin (2 Cor. 5:21; Gal. 3:13; Heb. 2:17). Now that God's requirement for justice has been met, He offers forgiveness for our sins. We receive His offer when we believe in Jesus (John 3:36; Acts 10:42-43; Rom. 5:9).

Christ's shed blood, which secured our forgiveness, also cleansed us from all sins (Heb. 9:22; 1 John 1:7b). This cleansing (or removal) was total and complete (Ps. 103:12; 1 Cor. 6:11; Heb. 10:12-18). At the moment of salvation, we are no longer dirty sinners soiled with sin; we are now clean, pure, and holy. Through the power of God's forgiveness, sins can never again make us dirty and unforgiven (Heb. 9:14). God's total forgiveness was the solution to problem #1 (our sinful behavior and guilt).

As a result of this forgiveness, we are reconciled to God (Rom. 5:10; 2 Cor. 5:18; Col. 1:20). Reconcile is also an accounting term that means to bring two accounts into agreement. Irreconcilable differences existed between God's demand for righteousness and humanity's accumulated sins (Matt. 5:48; Rom. 2:5). Through Christ's work on the cross, He reconciled these differences (2 Cor. 5:18-19; Eph. 2:16; Col. 2:13).

Now that we are reconciled to God, we are fully justified. In judicial terms, justified means to be declared not guilty. God's justification through Christ took away our guilt and declared our sin debt paid in full (Matt. 20:28; Col. 2:14; Heb. 9:26b). Nothing stands between God and us. We are no longer separated from Him because of sin. We have been brought close to God through the blood of Christ (Eph. 2:13).

CRUCIFIED AND RESURRECTED WITH CHRIST

What do the words "crucified with Christ" in Galatians 2:20 imply? When Christ hung on the cross and died, provision was made for the death of our old self as well (Col. 3:3). At the moment of belief, the old self (unrighteous identity) was spiritually placed into Christ and literally crucified with Him (Rom. 6:3-7). We were also buried with Him and raised with Him as a new creation (Eph. 2:6; Col. 2:12). This solved problem #2 (our old self and shame) and gave us, as believers, a new spirit and identity at the moment of our spiritual birth (Ezek. 36:26-27; John 3:3; 1 Pet. 1:23).

"I have been crucified with Christ; and it is no longer I who live, but Christ lives in me;" - Galatians 2:20a

ILLUSTRATION:
TWO SIDES OF THE CROSS

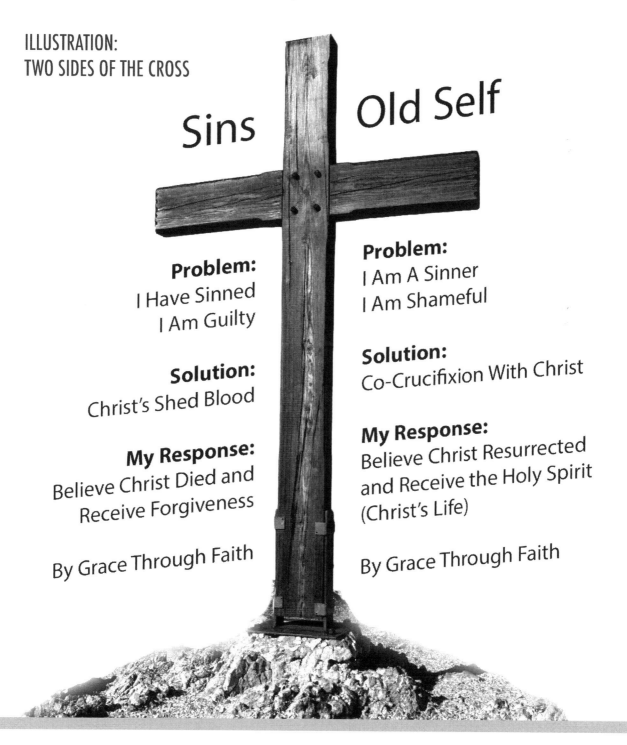

Sins

Old Self

Problem:
I Have Sinned
I Am Guilty

Solution:
Christ's Shed Blood

My Response:
Believe Christ Died and
Receive Forgiveness

By Grace Through Faith

Problem:
I Am A Sinner
I Am Shameful

Solution:
Co-Crucifixion With Christ

My Response:
Believe Christ Resurrected
and Receive the Holy Spirit
(Christ's Life)

By Grace Through Faith

OUR RESPONSE TO GOD'S SOLUTION

"that if you confess with your mouth Jesus as Lord, and believe in your heart that God raised Him from the dead, you shall be saved;" - Romans 10:9

God dealt with both of our problems on the cross, providing the way for us to know Him and live as He originally purposed. Now that He has done everything necessary, what is required on our part to enjoy His presence and life? The response God desires from every person is to believe in who He is, what He has done for us, then receive and embrace every gift that He has given us in Christ (John 3:15-18; 5:24; 6:29; 20:31; Acts 16:30-31; Rom. 1:16; 3:22-24; Gal. 3:22; Eph. 2:8). The moment we believe in our heart and confess with our mouth (Rom. 10:9-10), God places us spiritually in Christ where we are crucified, buried, and resurrected to new life. This work of God results in an identity change for the believer along with the benefits described in the next session, "The Great Exchange."

ILLUSTRATION: PLACED SPIRITUALLY INTO CHRIST

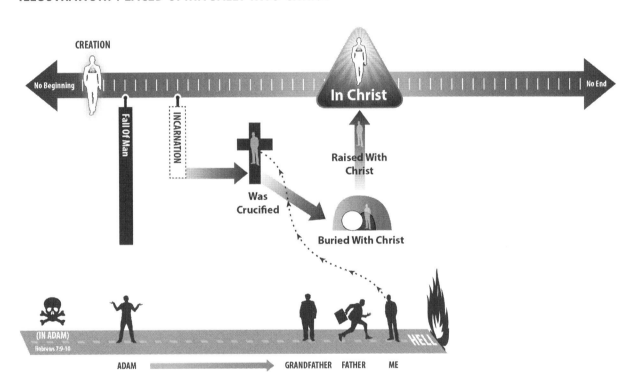

SUMMARY

God, in the person of Jesus, has resolved the two problems that kept us from an intimate relationship with Him. He dealt with our sins (problem #1) when He became flesh and blood, fulfilling the Law, and paid the penalty for sin through the sacrifice of Himself. He removed our fallen and natural identity in Adam (problem #2) by crucifying our old self in Christ. Our response is to believe and receive God's provision for our salvation.

TRANSFORM

1. Have I ever believed and received God's provision for my salvation? If yes, how did that happen?

   _____

   _____

   _____

   _____

   _____

   _____

   _____

   _____

   _____

2. How does it impact me to know I do not have to pay my sin debt?

   _____

   _____

   _____

   _____

   _____

   _____

   _____

3. In what ways does understanding my complete forgiveness change my experience of intimacy with God?

   _____

   _____

   _____

   _____

   _____

   _____

   _____

4. What does it mean that my "old self" was crucified with Christ?

_____

_____

_____

_____

_____

_____

_____

5. In what ways do I struggle with believing, receiving, and trusting God?

_____

_____

_____

_____

_____

_____

_____

_____

 **PRAY**

Dear Father, thank You for the precious gift of Your Son, Jesus. I know I am justified through the sacrifice of Your Son. In Him, You secured my righteousness, made me a new creation, and gave me Your life. Nothing is left for me to do except trust in Your provision, enter Your rest, and give thanks and praise. Thank You for forgiving ALL of my sins and putting to death my old, rebellious self. Your lovingkindness overwhelms me. Amen.

THE GREAT EXCHANGE
Restored Life

9

CONNECT

- What has God revealed to you since we last met?

- What does it mean that every person is born with a sin nature?

- In John 3:7 Jesus said, "You must be born again." What did He mean by "born again?"

- What is the role of the Holy Spirit in the believer?

RENEW

BECAME NEW CREATIONS

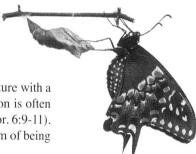

At our co-crucifixion with Christ, God replaced (exchanged) the old sinful nature with a new nature which is Christ's nature (2 Cor. 5:17; 2 Pet. 1:4). This new creation is often referred to as a saint (1 Cor. 1:2; Eph. 1:1), which is now our new identity (1 Cor. 6:9-11). The new saint is now free from the old, sinful nature and can live in the freedom of being in Christ (Rom. 6:6-11; 8:10; Gal. 2:20).

As saints, we have new hearts with new desires which align with God's heart and desires (Jer. 24:7; 31:33; Ezek. 36:26-27). Whereas the sinner with the sinful nature was naturally bent toward sin, now the saint with a new spirit is bent toward holiness and righteousness (Rom. 7:16, 22; Gal. 5:17). Thinking, feeling, choosing, and behaving righteously is the most natural thing for the new creation in Christ (Rom. 6:17-18; Gal. 5:24). Now that we have a new identity, our behavior can reflect who we are in Christ (Eph. 4:24).

Just as a butterfly is made new inside a chrysalis, so too believers are made new spiritually in Christ.

ENTERED THE NEW COVENANT

"But now He has obtained a more excellent ministry, by as much as He is also the mediator of a better covenant, which has been enacted on better promises." - Hebrews 8:6

What is the purpose of a covenant? A covenant is an agreement of conduct or relationship between two parties. The old covenant in Scripture was a conditional covenant (If... then...) based on man's performance (Ex. 19:3-5; Deut. 11:26-32; 19:3-5, 7-9; James 2:10). The new covenant is unconditional and based only on the performance of Christ (Is. 53:10-11; Matt. 26:28; Rom. 10:4; Heb. 9:1-28). Under the old covenant, men and women strove to produce righteousness through self-effort. Under the new covenant, believers are gifted righteousness (Rom. 5:17) and express it by surrendering to the Holy Spirit (1 Cor. 6:19-20). The old covenant is an achieving system; the new covenant is a receiving system.

Because Jesus made a new and better covenant with us than the one God made with Israel (Heb. 8:6), no amount of failures, mistakes, trials or tribulations can separate us from the life of God (Rom. 8:1, 31-39). This security is based on the finished work of Christ, not on our self-effort to be good (Eph. 2:8-9).

OBTAINED AN ETERNAL INHERITANCE

"And if you belong to Christ, then you are Abraham's descendants, heirs according to promise."
- Galatians 3:29

God made a covenant with Abraham and promised He would bless all nations through him (Gen. 12:2-3; 15:1-21). That blessing was the promised inheritance that would be distributed after the death of Christ (Gal. 3:8-9; Heb. 9:15-17) who was the covenant maker (John 8:58).

Everyone who is in Christ is an heir (Gal. 3:29). As an heir, we have inherited Christ's nature. At the moment of salvation, we inherit Christ's power and strength to express His life in this world (2 Cor. 12:9; Eph. 1:3; Phil. 4:13; 2 Pet. 1:3). We have also inherited an eternal home in heaven (1 Pet. 1:3-5). Much more remains to be explored concerning our inheritance because Ephesians 1:3 says, "He has blessed us with every spiritual blessing in the heavenly places in Christ."

INDWELT BY THE HOLY SPIRIT

"He who believes in Me, as the Scripture said, 'From his innermost being shall flow rivers of living water.' But this He spoke of the Spirit, whom those who believed in Him were to receive;"
- John 7:38, 39

At the moment of salvation, the Holy Spirit enters and indwells the believer (Rom. 8:9). What is the purpose of being indwelt by the Holy Spirit? Even though we are new creations with new natures, we still need life (John 10:10b). We are incapable of generating life for ourselves (John 15:5). Not even a forgiven, reconciled, and justified person can produce life. Only the Spirit gives life (John 6:63; 2 Cor. 3:6).

Before He ascended, eternal life was in Jesus (John 1:4; 1 John 5:11). He revealed to His disciples that He must go away so He could impart His life to them through the indwelling Holy Spirit (John 7:38-39; 16:7). This life entered them at Pentecost (Acts 1:4-5; 2:1-4).

The Holy Spirit not only gives life to the believer, but also is our helper (John 15:26; 16:7), our counselor (1 John 2:27), and our liberty (2 Cor. 3:17). He makes God's mind known to us (John 14:26; 16:13; 1 Cor. 2:10-13). He reminds us of our identity as God's children (Rom. 8:16). He intercedes for us (Rom. 8:26). The Holy Spirit is the source of Christ's power in us (Acts 1:8a; 2 Tim. 1:7).

SEALED BY THE HOLY SPIRIT

A seal is a device or substance that is used to join two things together to prevent them from coming apart or to prevent anything from passing between them. During the days of the Apostle Paul, wax seals were used not only to close letters and scrolls, but additionally to establish ownership and express authority. When we place our faith and trust in Jesus Christ, the Father sends His Spirit to live inside of us as a sign of His authority, of our belonging, and of the security that we will always live together with Him (1 Cor. 6:17; 2 Cor. 1:22; Eph. 1:13; 4:30). Once the Spirit is given to a believer by faith, He is never taken back (John 10:28). We are sealed forever (John 14:16).

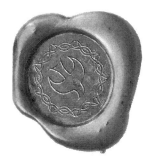

ILLUSTRATION: LIFE RESTORED BY JESUS CHRIST

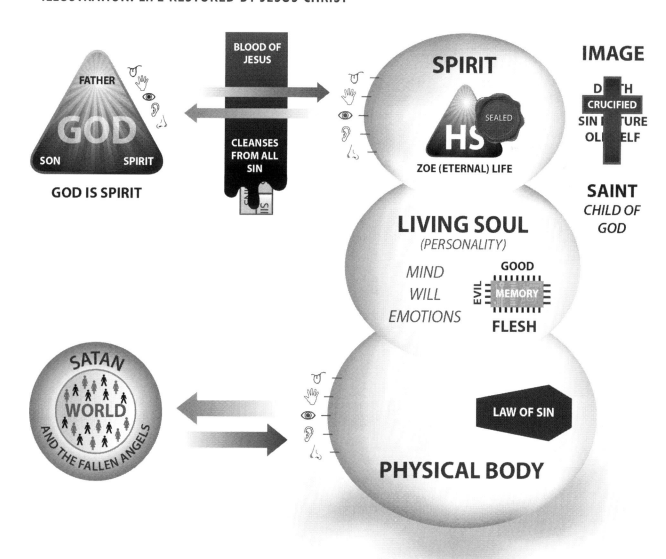

"And my God shall supply all your needs according to His riches in glory in Christ Jesus." - Philippians 4:19

NEEDS MET IN CHRIST

After the Fall, Adam and Eve attempted to meet their own needs apart from God by walking after their flesh. This futile way of life was passed from generation to generation. Through Christ's provision, God satisfies our deepest needs once again. Our need for love, acceptance, worth, and security are completely met as we believe and receive His provision. Christ's life in us (the Holy Spirit) is the infinite source given by the Father to meet our needs (Phil. 4:19).

Even our physical needs are important to God. Christ reminded us God takes care of the birds and the flowers, and we are worth more to Him than these (Matt. 6:25-33; Luke 12:22-32).

ILLUSTRATION: GOD'S PROVISION IN JESUS CHRIST

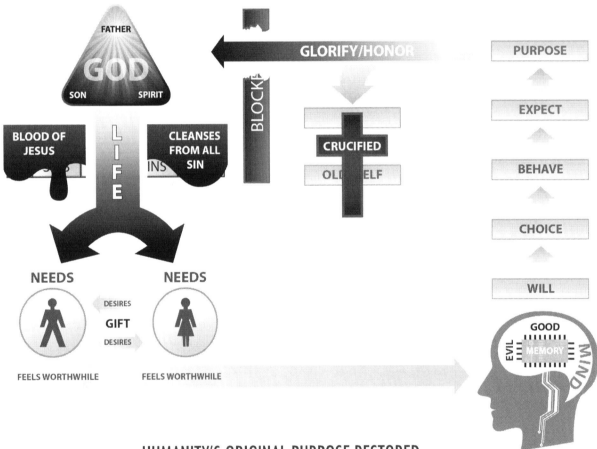

HUMANITY'S ORIGINAL PURPOSE RESTORED

Through Christ, our original purpose of containing and expressing God's life has been reestablished (Gen. 1:26a). We are now able to live out of Christ's life in us (1 John 4:9). When God told Adam to eat freely from any tree in the garden (Gen. 2:16), He gave Adam freedom to live out of His life. Now, through Christ, that same freedom has been restored (Gal. 5:1).

SUMMARY

At the moment of salvation, we were made new creations indwelt by the Holy Spirit, and we entered into a new covenant with God characterized by abundant life. The old, sinful nature (old self) was exchanged for a new nature so we can naturally and uniquely express Christ's life in every action. We were given a full, spiritual inheritance with the guarantee that all needs will be met in Christ.

TRANSFORM

1. Why does it bother me when I sin? What does that say about my true desires?

2. In what ways have I experienced the presence of the Holy Spirit in me?

3. What does abundant life mean to me?

4. What does it mean personally to be an entirely new being, a "new creation" made in the image of God?

_____

_____

_____

_____

_____

5. What have I inherited in Christ? Make a list.

_____	_____
_____	_____
_____	_____
_____	_____
_____	_____
_____	_____
_____	_____
_____	_____
_____	_____
_____	_____
_____	_____

 **PRAY**

Father, thank You for making me a new creation with a new nature. Thank You for giving me a new heart with new desires. Thank You for making me eternally secure by placing Your Holy Spirit in me. Thank You for making me an heir and blessing me with every spiritual blessing in Christ. Thank You for restoring life in me so that my thoughts, my emotions, my choices, and my behavior can express Your glory. Amen.

10

A NEW IDENTITY
Christ's Life

 CONNECT

- What has God revealed to you since we last met?

- How do you identify yourself?

- What do people typically rely on to identify themselves?

- In today's society, how do people change their identities? Why would they want a new identity?

- What does it feel like to go through an identity change?

- How does family affect identity?

 RENEW

FAMILY DETERMINES IDENTITY

Throughout history, family lineage has been a powerful source of identity. In most countries, people are identified by both a first and last name. The last name indicates the family lineage through the connection to the father.

Spiritually speaking, we are all born into the family of Satan (Eph. 2:1-3). He is our spiritual birth father (John 8:44; 1 John 3:10). When we come to Christ through faith, Scripture says

"But as many as received Him, to them He gave the right to become children of God, even to those who believe in His name,"

- John 1:12

INHERITING OUR RIGHTEOUS IDENTITY

It is made available as a gift through the love of Christ (Rom. 5:19).

It is revealed by grace through faith in love (Rom. 1:16-17; Phil. 3:8-9).

We receive it by faith as a love gift (Rom. 5:17).

It is confirmed by the Holy Spirit in love (John 16:8-11; Rom. 8:16-17a).

we exchange families by obtaining a new father (John 1:12; Gal. 3:26; 4:5-7; 1 John 4:4). This wonderful gift of God is adoption into His family (Rom. 8:15) which results in a radical change in our identity. We are now defined as dearly loved "children of God" (1 John 3:1a).

FULLY ACCEPTED

Everyone has the inner need for acceptance. Not only do we need to be accepted, but we also need to be accepted unconditionally with no strings attached to our performance, possessions, talents, or worldly status. As discussed in Session 3, only one source exists who can meet the need for that kind of acceptance - God (1 Cor. 8:6). His unconditional and complete acceptance of us is based on who He is and what He has done for us in Christ. When we were enemies of God, He pursued us and adopted us by His own initiative (John 1:13).

Righteousness equals acceptance in God's eyes. Through Jesus Christ, God made us righteous by giving us HIS righteousness (Rom. 5:17). The moment we accept His gift of righteousness, it belongs to us. Because we received Jesus' FULL righteousness on the day of our salvation (Rom. 3:22-24; Eph. 4:24; Col. 2:10), we are now righteous people. We are not borrowing Jesus' righteousness or hiding under (or behind) Jesus to gain God's acceptance. Righteousness (also known as purity or blamelessness) is not slowly and gradually attained by believers as they convert bad performance (sin) into good performance. Righteousness and God's full acceptance have been attained by Christ's work on our behalf, and righteous is now our new identity.

Now that we are accepted, we can readily draw near to Him (Heb. 4:16; 10:22). Because we are God's beloved children, our need for acceptance is fully met by our Heavenly Father. We will experience our acceptance when we know and believe that we are now His beloved (Eph. 5:1b; Col. 3:12; 1 John 4:16).

HOW RIGHTEOUS ARE WE?

Are we as righteous as the Apostle Paul? As righteous as Jesus? Since we have been given His (Christ's) righteousness, we are as righteous as Jesus Christ (Matt. 5:20; 1 Cor. 1:30-31; 1 John 4:17b). This righteousness is not by anything we have done, but by what Christ has done on the cross (Eph. 2:8-9). Righteous is now our nature (Rom. 6:18). We are not just accepted, we are acceptable (2 Cor. 5:21; Phil. 3:9; 1 Pet. 2:9; 2 Pet. 1:4).

ASPECTS OF OUR IDENTITY AS CHILDREN OF GOD

As a result of receiving the gift of God in Christ and adoption into His family, God reveals many aspects of our new identity. Now, let us take a closer look at some of these aspects.

GOD'S CHILD

"He predestined us to adoption as sons through Jesus Christ to Himself, according to the kind intention of His will," Ephesians 1:5

DEARLY LOVED

"See how great a love the Father has bestowed on us, that we would be called children of God; and such we are." 1 John 3:1

LOVED UNCONDITIONALLY

"For I am convinced that neither death, nor life, nor angels, nor principalities, nor things present, nor things to come, nor powers, nor height, nor depth, nor any other created thing, will be able to separate us from the love of God, which is in Christ Jesus our Lord." Romans 8:38-39

FRIEND OF JESUS

"No longer do I call you slaves, for the slave does not know what his master is doing; but I have called you friends," John 15:15

GOD'S PRECIOUS POSSESSION

"But you are a chosen race, a royal priesthood, a holy nation, a people for God's own possession, so that you may proclaim the excellencies of Him who has called you out of darkness into His marvelous light;" 1 Peter 2:9

BRIDE OF CHRIST

"Husbands, love your wives, just as Christ also loved the church and gave Himself up for her, so that He might sanctify her, having cleansed her by the washing of water with the word, that He might present to Himself the church in all her glory, having no spot or wrinkle or any such thing; but that she would be holy and blameless." Ephesians 5:25-27

GOD'S RESIDENCE

"Or do you not know that your body is a temple of the Holy Spirit who is in you, whom you have from God, and that you are not your own?" 1 Corinthians 6:19

NEW CREATION

"Therefore if anyone is in Christ, he is a new creature; the old things passed away; behold, new things have come." 2 Corinthians 5:17

VICTORIOUS

"But in all these things we overwhelmingly conquer through Him who loved us." Romans 8:37

PERFECTED, SANCTIFIED

"For by one offering He has perfected for all time those who are sanctified." Hebrews 10:14

BLAMELESS

"just as He chose us in Him before the foundation of the world, that we would be holy and blameless before Him." Ephesians 1:4

ADEQUATE

"I can do all things through Him who strengthens me." Philippians 4:13

Additional Reference:
2 Corinthians 3:5

NEVER ALONE

". . . for He Himself has said, "I will never desert you, nor will I ever forsake you." Hebrews 13:5

GOD'S WORKMANSHIP

"For we are His workmanship, created in Christ Jesus for good works, which God prepared beforehand so that we would walk in them." Ephesians 2:10

SUMMARY

At salvation, we exchanged fathers - from Satan to God. Changing fathers produced a family exchange - from Adam's family to God's family. Our identity is now a dearly loved child of God who is righteous and fully accepted. As God's children we have an identity that is defined by who HE is, by what HE has done, and by HIS opinion of us.

TRANSFORM

1. Which aspect(s) of my new identity do I most believe and enjoy?

    _____

    _____

    _____

    _____

2. Which aspect(s) of my new identity do I have the most trouble believing?

    _____

    _____

    _____

    _____

3. What do the *Aspects of Our Identity as Children of God* listed in this session say about God's opinion of me?

    _____

    _____

    _____

    _____

4. What could keep me from embracing the truth of who I am (God's opinion of me)?

    _____

    _____

    _____

    _____

5. What will my life look like if I do not believe God has changed my identity?

_____

_____

_____

_____

6. Take some time to listen. What is the Holy Spirit telling me in this session?

_____

_____

_____

_____

7. How will the Holy Spirit's revelation impact my beliefs, choices, and behaviors?

_____

_____

_____

_____

 **PRAYER**

Father, thank You for accomplishing everything You require for me to enjoy You. Thank You for adopting me into Your family with all the rights and privileges that come with being a joint heir with Christ. Thank You for doing everything necessary to obtain my righteousness and for giving it to me. It is not the result of anything I have done, but only what You have done and bestowed upon me. Holy Spirit, thank You for reminding me of who I am in Christ - God's child, fully righteous, accepted, loved, and capable of anything You lead me to do. Now that there is nothing wrong with me, I am free to trust Your love, lean into Your voice of grace, and express Your life and love to others. Amen.

INTIMACY WITH GOD
Fellowship with Life

CONNECT

- What has God revealed to you since we last met?

- Have you heard the voice of the Holy Spirit? How did you hear Him? What did He say?

- In what ways has the Holy Spirit spoken to you in the past?

- Why is there sometimes a struggle to hear from God?

RENEW

INTIMATE LIFE TOGETHER

As God's beloved children, we enjoy healthy family life with Him. Everything we do as believers is done with God (1 Cor. 6:15-17): eating (Rev. 3:20); working (Phil. 2:12-13); resting (Matt. 11:28); speaking (1 Pet. 4:11); praying (Rom. 8:26); etc.

As lovers of God, we desire to experience deeper intimacy with Him (1 Cor. 13:12; Eph. 3:18-19). Intimacy is close, loving, personal fellowship between people who know and trust each other. God created marriage to be an earthly illustration of our spiritual intimacy with Him (Ezek. 16:8; Eph. 5:25, 31-32). A man and woman grow in intimacy as they spend time together and learn more about each other.

God fully knows us (Ps. 139; Gal. 4:9a) and invites us to know Him (Jer. 29:13; Luke 10:27; John 17:22-24). At the moment of salvation, God's Spirit takes up residence inside us and enables us to know Him personally and enjoy intimate fellowship with Him (Jer. 31:33-34; Mark 12:30-31; John 14:16; 1 Cor. 2:10; Eph. 2:8; Col. 1:24-29).

". . . if anyone hears My voice and opens the door, I will come in to him and will dine with him, and he with Me."
- Revelation 3:20b

Intimacy grows only on a foundation of trust, and trust develops within a safe relationship. People provide relational safety when they love unconditionally, freely extend grace, encourage, speak truth in love, display kindness, are not easily angered, forgive quickly, show mercy, and demonstrate faithfulness.

Our God is completely safe (Ps. 16:1-2). His nature (Session 1) and His acceptance of us (Session 10) provide a solid foundation to experience deep intimacy with our Father and our Bridegroom (Jesus) through the Holy Spirit.

A DEPENDENT RELATIONSHIP BASED ON TRUST

Our life together with God is characterized by His leadership and our dependence. As we learn God's character (Session 1), we grow in trust. God is love (1 John 4:8), and He always chooses to work in our best interest (Jer. 29:11; Rom. 8:28; 1 Pet. 5:7). In response, we love, trust, and follow Him as He leads us (Gal. 5:6b; 1 John 5:3).

GOD LEADS US BY HIS VOICE

Scriptures frequently describe God and Jesus as the Good Shepherd who leads, guides, and protects His sheep (Gen. 48:15; Ps. 23:1; 95:7; Is. 40:11; John 10:11; 1 Pet. 2:25). God does not lead us with impersonal instructions or commands. Instead, He leads us with love into greater intimacy and empowers us by the Holy Spirit to follow Him (Session 9, "Indwelt by the Holy Spirit").

Just as a shepherd's voice is familiar to his sheep and they eagerly follow his call, so too the Holy Spirit's voice leads the children of God. Jesus said, "My sheep hear My voice, and I know them, and they follow Me" (John 10:27). Every child of God hears the voice of God and is led by the Holy Spirit (John 8:47; 18:37c; Rom. 8:4, 14). When we respond in faith to God's voice, we experience the supernatural fruit of the Spirit which fills us with hope (Rom. 15:13; Gal. 5:22-23). God speaks, and we grow in our ability to hear as we practice listening with obedience (Ps. 95:6-8; Heb. 5:11-14).

"...and the sheep hear his (the shepherd's) voice, and he calls his own sheep by name and leads them out. When he puts forth all his own, he goes ahead of them, and the sheep follow him because they know his voice." - John 10:3a-4

GOD'S VOICE IS UNIQUE

In the natural world every person's voice is unique in tone and pitch. As we listen to a person speak, their specific sound patterns register in our mind. Therefore, we can learn to identify another person just by hearing them speak. In addition to the tone and pitch, we also recognize a person's voice by their choice of words.

We learn spiritual voices in much the same way. As we spend intimate time with God in prayer (conversation) and Bible study, we learn the tone and pitch of His voice (John 10:4). God's voice sounds different from the voices of Satan and demons (John 10:5). Once we learn the sound of God's voice, we can recognize Him quickly when He speaks to our heart (1 Sam. 3:8-9).

GOD'S VOICE VS SATAN'S VOICE

GOD'S VOICE	SATAN'S VOICE
Speaks truth (John 17:17; Heb. 6:18)	**Speaks lies** (John 8:44)
Never tempts (James 1:13)	**Always tempts** (Matt. 4:1; 1 Cor. 7:5; 1 Thess. 3:5)
Leads us to love God and others (John 13:34)	**Entices us to act selfishly** (Matt. 4:3-8; Acts 5:3)
Is consistent (Num. 23:19; 1 Sam. 15:29; Heb. 13:8)	**Changes depending on the scheme** (2 Cor. 2:11; 11:14)
Brings Peace (Ps. 85:8; John 20:21; 1 Cor. 14:33; 2 Thess. 3:16)	**Stirs up confusion and fear** (Rom. 8:15; 2 Tim. 1:7)
Reminds us who we are in Christ (Is. 43:1; Rom. 8:16)	**Focuses on what we do** (Rev. 12:10)
Affirms (Is. 54:15; Jer. 31:3; Eph. 4:29)	**Accuses** (Job 1:9-11; 2:5; Zech. 3:1)
Testifies truthfully about Jesus (1 Cor. 12:3; 2 Cor. 10:5; 1 John 4:2)	**Slanders Jesus** (1 John 4:3)
Gently invites, sometimes whispers (1 Kin. 19:11-13; Is. 40:11; Matt. 11:28-30; Rev. 3:20)	**Demands and shouts** (Gen. 3:4; Matt. 4:6)
Trains us in righteousness with a focus on our future (Phil. 3:13; 2 Tim. 3:16; Heb. 12:6-11)	**Emphasizes our failures with a focus on the past** (1 Pet. 5:8)

BY WHAT MEANS DOES THE HOLY SPIRIT COMMUNICATE TO US?

The Holy Spirit speaks to us directly in our mind with thoughts, images, or impressions. He also communicates through the Scriptures, other people, and other means. Often God speaks through a combination of these ways. It is essential to cross-check any guidance we receive with the Bible. Whatever the form of communication, the Holy Spirit will never take away from, add to, or contradict the completed Scriptures (Num. 23:19; Gal. 1:8-9; Rev. 22:18-19). It is additionally helpful to seek Godly counsel (Prov. 1:5; 8:14; 13:10; 19:21) from a mature believer who is full of faith, understands Scripture, and knows the voice of God.

THROUGH HIS VOICE IN OUR MINDS AND SPIRITS

The Holy Spirit impacts our spirit and speaks truth into our mind (Luke 12:12; John 3:8; Rom. 8:16; 1 Cor. 2:10-13). Because He is spirit, He can stir our spirit (Ezra 1:1; Hag. 1:14). The inner spiritual voice of the Holy Spirit sounds like spontaneous thoughts coming into our mind (Matt. 10:19-20; 16:15-17). Some have described the impact of His voice as a revelation, a moment of clarity, or an inner knowing, which aligns with God's written Word and leads to peace, comfort, and assurance (2 Tim. 2:7). For example, many pastors and missionaries have received specific direction from the Holy Spirit to enter vocational ministry (Acts 13:1-3).

Satan and demons can tempt us to believe lies when we are making decisions (Luke 4:2; James 1:13). The enemy wants us to believe his lies are thoughts we generate, but the Holy Spirit speaks as a separate, distinguishable voice (John 14:17). We may receive an uneasiness or check in our spirit when making a decision, or alternately we may experience supernatural peace in our spirit (Rom. 9:1). Through discerning God's voice within us, we experience and enjoy the mind of Jesus Christ (1 Cor. 2:16).

THROUGH THE BIBLE

Throughout early history, the Holy Spirit inspired believers to write down the words God spoke to them (Amos 3:7; 2 Pet. 1:21) for the instruction of those born later (Rom. 15:4; 1 Cor. 10:11; 2 Tim. 3:16). The Bible contains a treasure of information about God's character, attributes, and heart (John 5:39) along with descriptions of the ways He communicated with people throughout history. The Holy Spirit is our teacher and guide (John 16:13; 1 John 2:27). As we read the Bible, the Holy Spirit highlights specific truths, instructions, or promises applicable to our current situation or struggles (1 Cor. 2:12-14). When the Holy Spirit speaks to us through Scripture, His words come with a strength, conviction, and confirmation within our spirit (Rom. 15:4; Heb. 4:12).

THROUGH OTHER PEOPLE

In the Old Testament, God spoke to the people through prophets stirred by the Holy Spirit (Num. 24:2; Judg. 3:10; 1 Sam. 10:6; Acts 1:16; Heb. 1:1a; 2 Pet. 1:21). Now, after Christ's resurrection, the Holy Spirit dwells in the hearts of God's people, where

He moves believers to encourage, comfort, and exhort one another (Matt. 10:20; 1 Cor. 14:3; Eph. 4:11-16, 29). He also uses others to proclaim the gospel (Acts 2:4; 4:31; Rom. 10:14-15), dispense wisdom and guidance (1 Cor. 12:4-11), and defend truth (Mark 13:11).

THROUGH OTHER MEANS

God has given His creation a voice to loudly proclaim His glory (Ps. 19:1-4; Rom. 1:19-20). Because He has uniquely created humans to enjoy His creation (Gen. 2:9), He reminds us of His words through what He has made (Job 12:7-10). God can remind us of His faithfulness through a rainbow (Gen. 9:12-16), or of His majesty through a large mountain (Nah. 1:5), or of His provision through a flower (Matt. 6:28-33).

God speaks through dreams and visions as well. In the Bible, many examples illustrate God speaking to people in these ways (Abraham - Gen. 15:1-7, 12-17; Jacob - Gen. 28:12; Joseph - Gen. 37:5-10; Daniel - Dan. 7:13-14; Joseph - Matt. 1:20-23; Peter - Acts 11:5-10; Paul - Acts 16:9; 18:9; John – Rev. 1:10; etc.). God still communicates with people today through dreams (while sleeping) and visions (while awake) (Acts 2:17).

On occasion, God uses angels to speak messages to humans (Luke 1:11-20, 26-38; Acts 9:26; 27:23-24). The word "angel" means messenger. Sometimes angels have appeared in visions and dreams (Ezek. 1:1-14; Matt. 1:20-21), other times they have manifested in physical form (Gen. 18; Dan. 9:21; Heb. 13:2). They will always represent God by speaking His words and carrying out His desires.

> "The heavens are telling of the glory of God; and their expanse is declaring the work of His hands. Day to day pours forth speech, and night to night reveals knowledge."
> - Psalms 19:1-2

A UNIQUE JOURNEY

God always pursues and intimately knows us. He reveals Himself to us through different means to invite us into greater dependency on and intimacy with Him. The enemy may tempt us to compare our communications from God with how He has spoken to His other children. This comparison can lead to a false belief of inferiority or superiority (Rom. 2:11). Satan wants us to try to get life (worth, value, meaning, purpose, etc.) from the means of communication (appearance of an angel or an audible voice). Each of us is on a unique, personal journey of intimacy with God. He wants us to passionately enjoy Him however He speaks to us (Ps. 16:11).

SUMMARY

God desires a close relationship with His children because He is love. Our lives together with God are characterized by His leadership and our dependence. He leads us through love into greater intimacy with Him and empowers us (through the Holy Spirit), to follow Him through the Holy Spirit. God fosters intimacy with us by speaking to us with His loving voice through the Holy Spirit. As we spend time with God in prayer and in the Scriptures, we learn to distinguish His voice from the voices of Satan and his demons. The Holy Spirit speaks to us directly in our minds by giving us thoughts, images, or impressions. He also communicates through the Scriptures, other people, and other means. Each of us is on a unique personal journey of life with God.

⊕ TRANSFORM

1. Why do I sometimes struggle with hearing God?

    _____
    _____
    _____
    _____
    _____
    _____
    _____
    _____

2. Set apart time this week to listen to God. Ask Him what He wants to say to you. As you receive a thought or impression, test it with the following questions:

    a. How is it consistent with Scripture?

        _____
        _____
        _____
        _____
        _____

    b. How does it align with God's voice versus Satan's voice? (See "God's Voice VS Satan's Voice")

        _____
        _____
        _____
        _____
        _____

c.   Is it producing peace, comfort, and assurance or fear, doubt, and anxiety?

_____

_____

_____

_____

_____

_____

3.   How will the Holy Spirit's revelation impact my beliefs, choices, and behaviors?

_____

_____

_____

_____

_____

_____

_____

_____

 **PRAYER**

Father, thank You for pursuing intimate fellowship with me. My heart soars when I hear Your voice inviting, encouraging, and affirming me in so many ways. Thank You for giving me spiritual ears so I can hear You speak personally with me. You know me fully, and I desire to intimately know You. Teach me to hear You in every moment and through whatever means You choose to use. Give me discernment to know Your voice and distinguish it from the other voices I hear. Share with me Your thoughts, wisdom, and plans. As my Good Shepherd, continue to lead me in love. As Your sheep, I desire to submit quickly to Your every prompting. Amen.

EXPRESSIONS OF HIS LIFE
Displaying Life

12

CONNECT

- What has God revealed to you since we last met?

- What do you think gives our Heavenly Father the most pleasure?

- How does Christ express His life on earth today?

- What characteristics are most evident when His life is expressed?

- How is the fruit of the Spirit produced in a believer's life?

RENEW

CREATED NEW TO BEAR FRUIT

The Father gets great glory and pleasure from seeing Christ's life displayed in our behavior (Session 4). Jesus calls this fruit bearing (John 15:8-9). God did the work of reconciling us to Himself. He paid the price for our sin so He could gift us His righteousness by faith. He crucified our old nature to raise us as new creations. God gifted us His Holy Spirit and sealed us in Him (Sessions 8 and 9). He did all that so we might bear fruit (Titus 3:3-8).

God often compares those who have been sanctified (made holy), for His purposes, to fruit bearing plants (e.g. a grape vine, fruit trees) (Matt. 12:33; John 15:5). He fully expects what He plants to bear fruit. Bearing fruit means to yield positive results. It can also mean to be successful, profitable, and effective. Every believer will produce fruit (John 15:8b).

> "You did not choose Me but I chose you, and appointed you that you would go and bear fruit, and that your fruit would remain, so that whatever you ask of the Father in My name He may give to you." - John 15:16

God's indwelling Spirit is the source of our life and, therefore, the source of our fruit (1 Cor. 3:16; 2 Cor. 3:6b; Phil. 1:11). When we choose to submit our mind to His thoughts and submit our will to His leading, we let His life and light shine through our actions (Matt. 5:16). The Bible describes God's life shining through us as fruit which glorifies Him (Eph. 5:9).

SPIRITUAL FRUIT

The Bible describes many different characteristics of the Spirit's expression of God's life in His children (Eph. 5:9; Phil. 1:11; Col. 1:11). Galatians 5:22-23 reveals nine characteristics. Generosity is included here as an application of goodness.

LOVE

God is love (1 John 4:8). God's life in us empowers us to unconditionally and supernaturally act in the best interest of every person who comes into our life (Rom. 5:5; 1 Cor. 13:4-7; 2 Cor. 5:14).

JOY

God's life brings with it a state of gladness that comes not from our circumstances, but from the love and grace of God poured into our hearts (Ps. 16:11). Joy can be contrasted with happiness in that joy comes from God's life in a believer (generated internally) and happiness depends on what happens to us (generated from outward circumstances) (Ps. 33:21; Rom. 15:13; Col. 1:11).

PEACE

God is peace (Judg. 6:24). His Spirit in us imparts a wholeness and restfulness to our soul as we cast all our cares, worries, fears, and anxieties on Him, knowing that He cares for us deeply (Is. 26:3; John 14:27; 16:33; Phil. 4:6-8; 1 Pet. 5:7). Peace is not the absence of conflict or adverse circumstances. Peace comes from God's presence, provision, total acceptance of us as believers, and promise that He will cause everything to work together for our good (Rom. 8:28).

PATIENCE

God is patient in that He is slow to anger and waits peacefully for His outcomes (Ex. 34:6; 2 Pet. 3:9). In us, He is our ability to wait on others and be slow to anger when we are offended (Col. 1:11).

KINDNESS

God is kind. He is always looking out for and considering the needs of others (Ex. 34:7a; 1 Chr. 16:34; Rom. 2:4). With His Spirit in us, we also have the ability to help and encourage others (Eph. 4:32; Col. 3:12; 1 Thess. 5:11, 14). God desires to see humanity express His kindness (Prov. 3:3-4; 19:22a).

GOODNESS / GENEROSITY

God is good. He is inherently righteous, decent, principled, and virtuous (Ps. 100:5; 136:1; Mark 10:17-18). He always leads us to do what is right or good. As we submit to the Holy Spirit, our words and actions will be good (Matt. 12:33-35; Rom. 15:14; Eph. 5:9; 1 Tim. 6:18).

In His goodness, God is generous. He owns everything (Deut. 10:14; Ps. 24:1; 50:12) and freely and joyfully shares His resources with us (Ps. 36:7-8; Matt. 5:45; John 3:16; 2 Cor. 8:9; 1 Tim. 6:17). As God's beloved stewards, we freely and cheerfully share His resources under the direction and power of the Holy Spirit (Ps. 112:9; Matt. 10:8b; Acts 2:44-45; Rom. 12:13; 2 Cor. 9:7- 11; 1 Tim. 6:18-19; Heb.13:16; 1 John 3:17).

FAITHFULNESS

God is faithful and always keeps His promises. He is 100% reliable (Num. 23:19; Lam. 3:22-23; 2 Tim. 2:13; Heb. 10:23). When we walk by the Spirit, we exude faithfulness to God, to ourselves, and to other people (Eph. 1:1; Col. 1:2).

GENTLENESS

Jesus showed us the gentleness of God (Matt. 11:29). He showed a humble meekness that was not weakness. As we live out of Christ's life, we will show calmness and tender care, considering others better than ourselves (Eph. 4:2; 1 Thess. 2:7; Titus 3:2; 1 Pet. 3:4, 15).

SELF-CONTROL (CONTROL OF SELF)

Jesus displayed perfect self-control. He was tempted in every way, yet He submitted to the Father and never sinned (John 5:19-20, 30; Heb. 4:15). The indwelling Holy Spirit sets us free from being mastered by fleshly desires (temptations). We have the power to say no to sin and yes to God (2 Tim. 1:7; Titus 2:11-14; 2 Pet. 1:5-9).

In Session 1 we discovered that God is love. When we look at His fruit, we see it all as different manifestations of His love.

"Love is patient, love is kind and is not jealous; love does not brag and is not arrogant, does not act unbecomingly; it does not seek its own, is not provoked, does not take into account a wrong suffered, does not rejoice in unrighteousness, but rejoices with the truth; bears all things, believes all things, hopes all things, endures all things."
- 1 Corinthians 13:4-7

WHERE DOES THE ABILITY TO BEAR FRUIT ORIGINATE?

The full ability of a branch to bear fruit comes from the flowing life of the vine. The grape vine does not produce fruit as a result of strain or effort by the branch. The grapes are produced quite naturally and spontaneously as the branch is connected to the vine, and the life of the vine continues to freely flow through the branch. A branch detached from the vine (a non-believer) can strive to produce grapes through self-effort, but will accomplish nothing. Therefore, it is fit only for burning (John 15:6).

In the same way, a noticeable distinction appears between those who are alive because they are in Christ (the branch connected to the vine) and those who are dead spiritually (the unattached branch) (Rom. 7:4-5). The Bible says we can tell by a person's fruit if they are abiding (born again with the Spirit of God inside them) (Matt. 7:16-20; 12:33; John 13:35; 15:5).

"I am the vine, you are the branches; he who abides in Me, and I in him, he bears much fruit; for apart from Me you can do nothing."
- John 15:5

"Then the King will say to those on His right, 'Come, you who are blessed of My Father, inherit the kingdom prepared for you from the foundation of the world. For I was hungry, and you gave Me something to eat; I was thirsty, and you gave Me something to drink; I was a stranger, and you invited Me in; naked, and you clothed Me; I was sick, and you visited Me; I was in prison, and you came to Me.'" - Matthew 25:34-36

WHO BENEFITS FROM FRUIT BEARING?

Fruit trees produce fruit for the benefit of others. In the same way, we bear the Spirit's fruit in order to bless, encourage, and build up others.

The Spirit's fruit in us benefits people who have not yet received eternal life. As we bear fruit, we give the wonderful flavor of life to those living a bland, difficult, or hopeless existence (Mark 9:50). This fruit offers an opportunity for the lost to "taste and see that the Lord is good" (Ps. 34:8).

In the natural world, a plant uses fruit as the vehicle to disperse its seeds and thereby reproduce itself. In the same way, God uses our spiritual fruit to reproduce His life and grow His kingdom. Inside the tasty fruit are the seeds of truth about God's life and love. Jesus said if we faithfully plant truth seeds, He causes them to grow into fruit bearing plants (Mark 4:26-29; 1 Cor. 3:6-7).

Our fruit production also benefits our brothers and sisters in Christ. To this end, God gifts every believer special talents, abilities, resources, and spiritual gifts so we will uniquely express Christ's life (1 Cor. 12:7; Eph. 4:11-13). When we express His life to other believers, we inspire them and build them up in their faith (Heb. 3:13). For example, a timely word can spur others to produce more fruit by reminding them of their new identity and encouraging them to listen to the Holy Spirit (Eph. 4:29; Heb. 10:24).

MAXIMIZING FRUIT PRODUCTION

Just as some branches bear more fruit than others, so also some Christians display more fruit of the Spirit than other believers (Matt. 13:23). If believers become distracted by the worries, riches, and pleasures of this life, they will walk after the flesh and bear less fruit (Luke 8:14). God, as our Gardner, desires to maximize fruit production in our lives (John 15:1-6, 8; Phil. 1:6; 2:13) by cultivating us to better receive His truth (Rom. 12:2; Heb. 12:2a). The Holy Spirit continually nourishes by reminding us of the reality of who God is, our true identity, and our relationship in Christ (John 14:26). As we believe these truths, we will bear fruit (Prov. 23:7a; Col. 1:10). Sometimes we do not heed His voice and choose to walk after the flesh. In those moments, He disciplines us as a loving Father (Heb. 12:6-11). His discipline is always for our good and teaches us to rely on Him (Jer. 29:11).

SUMMARY

God designed us to uniquely express Christ's life. The Bible calls this expression "bearing fruit." Christ's life in each of us is our life. It flows from us naturally and spontaneously as we submit our will to His. Every believer is endowed with unique talents, abilities, and spiritual gifts. These enable the believer to individually express Christ's life for the benefit and edification of Christ's body - the church. Our expression of Christ's life is most evident when we focus on the truth and enjoy intimacy with the Father.

TRANSFORM

1. What does my expression of Christ's life look like?

   _____

   _____

   _____

   _____

   _____

   _____

   _____

   _____

   _____

2. Describe a recent situation where I bore fruit. Who benefitted?

   _____

   _____

   _____

   _____

   _____

   _____

   _____

   _____

   _____

3. What keeps me from expressing His life?

   _____

   _____

   _____

   _____

   _____

   _____

   _____

4. Take some time to listen. What is the Holy Spirit telling me in this session?

_____

_____

_____

_____

_____

_____

_____

_____

5. How will the Holy Spirit's revelation impact my beliefs, choices, and behaviors?

_____

_____

_____

_____

_____

_____

_____

_____

_____

 **PRAY**

Father, I passionately desire to bear the fruit of Your Spirit. Thank You for giving me everything I need to bear fruit in its season. When I am setting my mind and trusting You to meet my needs, the most natural thing is to consider others more important than myself. Thank You for maximizing the production of fruit in my life in order to reveal Christ's beautiful life in me. Amen

13

GROWING IN GRACE AND KNOWLEDGE
Cultivating Life

CONNECT

- What has God revealed to you since we last met?

- What is spiritual growth?

- What causes spiritual growth?

- What motivates you to pray and read your Bible?

- What kind of things build intimacy with God?

RENEW

WHAT IS SPIRITUAL GROWTH?

The Bible frequently describes people in agricultural terms (Ps. 1:3). Some striking similarities exist between plants and people. In the last session, we looked at how both plants and believers can bear fruit. In addition, both start young and small and then grow over time to maturity.

The Bible describes our spiritual lives in much the same way as our physical bodies. When the truth germinates in our heart by faith, new life springs forth by the implanting of the Spirit inside our spirit. At the moment of our spiritual birth, we have everything we need for life and godliness (2 Pet. 1:3), and yet we are described as immature babies. Spiritual babies are defined as those who are still operating primarily out of their programmed flesh (1 Cor. 3:1-3) (Session 7). From the moment we are born again, God desires each of His new children to grow in His grace so that the life of Christ might be

The life of a mighty oak tree is in the little acorn. It only needs watering and nourishing for it to grow to full potential.

"I planted, Apollos watered, but God was causing the growth. So then neither the one who plants nor the one who waters is anything, but God who causes the growth."
- 1 Corinthians 3:6-7

manifested completely through our every word and deed (Eph. 4:15; 2 Pet. 3:18). Mature believers walk by the Spirit and live consistently from the inside out (Session 4).

WHO CAUSES THE GROWTH?

Scripture tells us it is God who does the work in us and causes us to grow (1 Cor. 3:5-7; Phil. 1:6; 2:13). He is the power. His words are the nourishment. It is the fruit of His life we carry.

The Bible is clear, however, that we do have a role to play in our growing process from spiritual babies to mature believers. Our part is to tend the internal garden by seeking out greater and greater intimacy with God so we can know His heart and quickly and clearly recognize His voice (John 10:27; Heb. 5:14; 1 John 2:13-14) (Session 11). As we hear His voice leading us, we can choose to submit our wills to His will. His light then shines forth in us for His glory (Matt. 5:16).

"...discipline yourself for the purpose of godliness..."
- 1 Timothy 4:7a

HOW DO WE PURSUE INTIMACY WITH GOD?

Healthy relationships are not one-sided. God's attention is always fixated on the objects of His love – us (1 Pet. 3:12). He desires us to engage in a personal relationship and intimate fellowship with Him. He constantly pursues us in order to gain our attention. If we are to live from, enjoy, and express His life, we too must tune our spiritual ears to His voice and in faith look to Him to meet all our needs (John 10:3-5).

The Bible talks of different ways we can foster intimacy with God. Some people over the millennia have referred to these as spiritual disciplines. It is important to note that we do not engage in these disciplines to earn God's acceptance or to achieve righteousness through self-effort (Eph. 2:8-9). God has already granted both to us. Spiritual disciplines, when carried out under the direction of the Holy Spirit, are opportunities to foster intimacy with God.

"like newborn babes, long for the pure milk of the word, that by it you may grow in respect to salvation," - 1 Peter 2:2

BIBLE STUDY

The importance of the Bible cannot be overstated. The Spirit will continually prompt us to read, study, memorize, and meditate on the Scriptures. The Bible is His sword for battle. He animates it and brings verses to mind at the moment of temptation (John 14:26; Eph. 6:17). Our assurance in Jesus grows as we study and meditate on the Bible with the Holy Spirit as our guide (John 16:13; Rom. 10:17).

The word of God is true and God-breathed (Prov. 30:5; John 17:17; 2 Tim. 3:16). As such, the Bible is a vast store of insight into God's character and nature. The word of God is sustenance for our soul and food for our spiritual growth and development (Matt. 4:4; John 6:63; Rom. 15:4; 2 Tim. 3:16-17). By spending time in God's word, we renew our mind with the truth, which in turn transforms our behavior and propels us to maturity (John 8:31-32; Rom. 12:2).

All the great people of faith revealed in the Bible enjoyed intimacy with God and a detailed knowledge of God's recorded words. King David took great delight in meditating on the Scriptures day and night (Ps. 1). In many of His sermons, Jesus simply expounded the Old Testament Scriptures. He exclusively used verses from the Bible to counter the temptations of Satan (Matt. 4:1-11). Jesus stated that the Scriptures themselves do not give life, but they point to Him, who IS our life (John 5:39-40; Col. 3:4).

WORSHIP

Worship is showing reverence or adoration for God. The foundation of worship is truth about God (John 4:23–24). As we get to know Him, we discover more and more the overwhelming, awe-inspiring wonders of His being. Worship begins in our heart (Ps. 86:12; Eph. 5:19) by treasuring God above all and lovingly submitting to His leading (Ps. 95:6-7). It is then expressed through our words, songs, and deeds (Rom. 12:1). For a believer, worship is a continual process as we express thanks and praise to Him throughout the day (Ps. 71:8; Heb. 13:15–16).

Because God designed us as social beings, we are blessed when we worship God with other believers (Col. 3:16). Hearing others praise, honor, and give thanks to God brings us joy and grows our faith in our Heavenly Father (Ps. 34:2-3).

"Come, let us worship and bow down, let us kneel before the LORD our Maker. For He is our God, and we are the people of His pasture and the sheep of His hand." - Psalms 95:6-7a

PRAYER

It is impossible to have a relationship without communication. Prayer is another name for conversing with God. Time spent in prayer is an opportunity for two-way communication with God on an intimate and personal level. The motivation to enter communion with God is love and the belief that He both hears and answers our prayers (1 Pet. 3:12; 1 John 5:14-15).

Because God knows everything about us, we can come before Him in complete honesty and transparency with the assurance that He is not disappointed in us or judging us (Rom. 8:1; Heb. 4:16; 10:22). We can also take comfort that God, in Christ, can identify with all our struggles (Heb. 2:18; 4:15). The Bible tells us to pray at all times about everything (Eph. 6:18; 1 Thess. 5:17). Sometimes the Spirit will lead us into enjoyable, intimate times of dedicated prayer much like two people who are dating look for times when they can be alone together (Song of Sol. 2:10; Matt. 6:6). While on earth, Jesus got up early and withdrew so He could regularly have those special times with His Father (Matt. 14:23; Mark 1:35).

Ephesians 2:10 says we were created for good works, and those works are expressions of Christ's life in us. Through times of prayer or conversation, we can listen to God as He gives direction, leading us to participate with Him as He expresses His life or glory in us. On Paul's second missionary journey he wanted to go to Bithynia, but the Spirit did not permit him to go. The Spirit wanted him to go to Macedonia instead (Acts 16:6-10). Paul had to listen in order to know what the Spirit desired and then submit his will to the Spirit's leading.

"With all prayer and petition pray at all times in the Spirit, and with this in view, be on the alert with all perseverance and petition for all the saints," - Ephesians 6:18

FASTING

Fasting is the ancient practice of denying the physical body something needed such as food and water and using the physical craving to focus the mind on the spiritual world (Col. 3:2). Fasting has been an integral part of the lives of saints for thousands of years. Scripture contains many examples of people who were led to fast: King David (Ps. 69:10), Ezra (Ezra 8:23), Nehemiah (Neh. 1:4), Daniel (Dan. 9:3), Jesus (Luke 4:2), Paul and Barnabas (Acts 14:23), etc.

Fasting should never be viewed as a way to manipulate God to fulfill our will or a way to earn the praise of man (Matt. 6:16-18). Instead, the Spirit will lead us to fast in order to reveal truth and bring us into greater intimacy with the Father. The temporary denial of a need can bring into sharp focus our dependence on God to meet our needs and the fact that we do not "live by bread alone, but by every word that proceeds from the mouth of God" (Deut. 8:3).

GIVING THANKS

Thanksgiving is an expression of gratitude that flows from the recognition that something valuable and good has been unconditionally given to us. As we walk with God, the Holy Spirit reveals to us all the good gifts we possess in Christ (John 16:14-15; 1 Cor. 2:9-10; James 1:17). When we respond by giving thanks, we experience the fruit of His peace and joy (Phil. 4:6-7).

Humanity's separation from God began by failing to recognize Him as provider and responding with thanks for all His good gifts (Rom. 1:21). Therefore, it follows that continual thanksgiving is an integral part of a healthy, intimate relationship with our generous God (Ps. 92:1; Eph. 5:20). God delights to give good gifts to us (Matt. 7:11). Giving thanks is one way we show our delight in receiving from Him (Heb. 11:6; 12:28). Jesus is our model for approaching every circumstance with gratitude. Before feeding hungry people, Jesus gave thanks (Mark 8:6). Before raising Lazarus from the dead, Jesus gave thanks (John 11:41). Before going to the cross, Jesus gave thanks (1 Cor. 11:24).

In 1 Thessalonians 5:18, Paul tells us it is God's will for us to give thanks in all things. In order to give thanks, we must first renew our minds by thinking about God and all the good He gives us. This process transforms our attitude into gratefulness which leads to expressions of thanksgiving (Rom. 12:2).

During times of temptation, approaching everything with gratitude is a powerful way to fight the lies of the enemy. It is impossible to express thanks to God for His provisions and covet someone else's possessions at the exact same time. Meditating on God's promises and responding with thankfulness works powerfully to extinguish the lies that lead to resentment, condemnation, and regret (Eph. 6:16).

OTHER DISCIPLINES

In the Bible, the Spirit also uses other ways to encourage our spiritual growth. The Bible instructs us to get together regularly with other believers for the purpose of fellowship, prayer, and encouragement in the truth (Acts 2:42; Col. 3:16; 1 Thess. 5:11; Heb. 10:25).

The world competes for our mental attention with its noisy distractions (televisions, phones, tablets, radios, computers, etc.) Sometimes the Holy Spirit will urge us to solitary and silent places so we can commune with God without distractions and hear His voice without competition (Matt. 14:23; Luke 5:15-16).

SUMMARY

While our spiritual growth is caused by God, we can foster this growth through spiritual disciplines which include Bible study, worship, prayer, fasting, giving thanks, etc. These activities provide opportunities to deepen our intimacy with God. We do not engage in them in order to earn God's acceptance or to achieve righteousness through self-effort. Spiritual disciplines, when carried out under the direction of the Holy Spirit, become ways of enjoying His presence and a means of knowing Him more intimately.

 **TRANSFORM**

1. In what ways do I enjoy intimacy with God?

   _____

   _____

   _____

2. Think about a special time with God in prayer or Bible study. What made it special?

   _____

   _____

   _____

3. As I spend intentional time fostering intimacy with God (Bible study, meditation, prayer, etc.), what have I noticed about my attitude regarding God? Myself? Other people? Life situations?

   _____

   _____

   _____

4. If I do not connect with other believers, how will that affect my growth?

   _____

   _____

   _____

   _____

5. Take some time to listen. What is the Holy Spirit telling me in this session?

_____

_____

_____

_____

_____

_____

6. How will the Holy Spirit's revelation impact my beliefs, choices, and behaviors?

_____

_____

_____

_____

_____

_____

 **PRAY**

Father, thank You for giving me Your Spirit and leading me moment by moment. Thank You for the Bible and for how You reveal Yourself to me as I spend time with You in Your Word. Thank You for granting me constant access to Your ear. Thank You that I can boldly approach Your throne of grace with thanksgiving, praise, and requests. I am overwhelmed as I realize You enjoy our time together. May I be ever sensitive to the Holy Spirit and obedient to Your promptings. As You lead me into opportunities to know You better through spiritual disciplines, use those moments to enlighten the eyes of my heart. Thank You for growing and maturing me as I act more out of who I am in Christ. I rest in the truth that You will lovingly complete the work You began in me. Amen.

THE BELIEVER'S BATTLE
Reigning in Life

14

CONNECT

- What has God revealed to you since we last met?

- Where do your thoughts originate?

- What is spiritual warfare?

- How do you know when you are under spiritual attack?

RENEW

IF WE ARE NEW CREATIONS AND HAVE THE HOLY SPIRIT, WHY DO WE STILL SIN?

God did not remove our mind, will, and emotions at salvation. In addition, He did not eliminate our programmed flesh patterns (Session 7) or remove the principle of sin in our physical body (Session 6). Our memories were not erased and our old habit patterns produced while we lived apart from Him were not reset. Instead, God gave us salvation, a new identity, new Godly desires, life in Christ, and freedom from sin. As noted in Session 9, He restored the ability and supplied the power to contain and express His life (enjoy intimate fellowship with God and glorify Him).

As new creations in Christ, we have the desire, choice, and provision to operate by faith and dependence to carry out the purpose for which we were designed (Sessions 9 and 10). When we discussed humanity's purpose before the Fall in Session 4, we called this "living from the inside out."

". . . though you were slaves of sin, you became obedient from the heart to that form of teaching to which you were committed, and having been freed from sin, you became slaves of righteousness." - Romans 6:17-18

By putting on Christ, we have all the spiritual armor we need (Gal. 3:27; Eph. 6:12-15). Jesus is our belt of truth (John 14:6). Jesus is our breastplate of righteousness (1 Cor. 1:30). Jesus is our peace, and His gospel brings peace (Col. 1:20). He is our shield of faith (Heb. 12:2). Jesus is our helmet of salvation (Acts 4:10-12). He is the living sword or Word of God (John 1:1).

However, we can also choose to listen to lies that encourage us to look to other people, objects, or experiences, to meet our needs. Believing these lies leads us to selfish actions (sin), which, in turn, produce misery, conflict, frustration, anxiety, and destruction (Gal. 5:19-21; James 4:1-2). In Session 6, we labeled this as "living from the outside in."

Day by day and moment by moment believers have the same choice Adam once had as he stood gazing at the tree of life and the tree of the knowledge of good and evil. Do we listen to the voice of the Holy Spirit, renew our mind with the truth that God meets all our needs, and live from the inside out (Rom. 12:2)? Or, do we believe the lies of our enemy (Eph. 6:16b; Rev. 12:9) and choose to live from the outside in? Will we walk by the Spirit or walk after the flesh (Gal. 5:16-17)?

If we choose to believe lies and walk after the old, selfish, fleshly ways, we will sin and reap the consequences in this life (Gal. 6:7-8; James 1:15). Everything we produce out of the flesh will be worthless and burned up in the last day (1 Cor. 3:12-15; Gal. 5:19-21; 2 Pet. 3:10). However, because the Holy Spirit is sealed in us (Session 9), we do not face eternal death when we commit a sin (John 6:39; 1 Thess. 5:9; Heb. 7:25; 9:12, 15).

ARE WE REALLY AT WAR?

The name Satan is from the Greek word "Satanas," which simply means "adversary." He actively tries to thwart the works of God in the world. Another name for him is "the devil," which means "slanderer" (false accuser). He unjustly accuses people in order to hurt and condemn. As people agree with his accusations, relationships are broken. Satan is a murderer and a liar (John 8:44). He desires the death and destruction of all humanity (1 Pet. 5:8). He actively lays traps (1 Tim. 3:7) and hatches schemes for the destruction of all people (2 Cor. 2:11). He is a prince (Eph. 2:2) and has been given permission to rule and control the world system (John 16:11) with his army of demons (Matt. 12:24; Luke 8:27-30; Eph. 6:11-12). Jesus summarized it by saying Satan came to kill, steal, and destroy (John 10:10a).

While Jesus freed believers from the penalty of sin (Session 8) and the control of Satan (Heb. 2:14; 1 Pet. 2:24), He has not removed Satan and his demons from this earth or removed the option to sin. Whether we realize it or not, we are at war with spiritual forces who seek our destruction (Eph. 6:12). Satan cannot kill the abundant life in a child of God, but he works through deception to hinder a child of God from experiencing and expressing God's abundant life (Heb. 3:13).

WHICH SIDE ARE WE ON?

At the moment of salvation, we left Satan's family and joined God's family (Session 10). That truth means we changed camps in a war (Col. 1:13). Before, we were friends with Satan and at war with God (Rom. 5:10; Eph. 2:1-3; Col. 1:21-22). Now we are friends with God and at war with Satan and his forces (1 Pet. 5:8). The good news is God already won the war at the cross (Eph. 1:19-22; Col. 2:13-15; 1 John 4:4). However, while we live on this earth, battles remain for us to fight (John 16:33).

WHERE DO THE BATTLES TAKE PLACE?

The battles we fight take place in our mind (2 Cor. 11:3; 1 Pet. 1:13). Even if it appears we are fighting with another person, in reality, we only battle the lies in our minds (2 Cor. 10:4; Eph. 6:12). These lies come from spiritual forces at work in the world. The world is under Satan's control, and it likewise feeds us lies and illusions (James 3:14-15; 1 John 5:19) through media, culture, people, education, etc.

God, through the Holy Spirit (Session 11), places thoughts into our minds (Matt. 16:17; John 10:27; 14:26; Acts 8:29). The demonic forces and the world can also introduce lies into our minds (Matt. 16:23; John 13:2; Acts 5:3). The enemy tempts us at opportune times by connecting his lies to our human desires (Luke 4:13; Eph. 4:26-27; James 1:14; 1 John 2:15-16). These evil thoughts are like flaming missiles. When they hit us, they light a fire in our emotions if not extinguished by believing the truth (Eph. 6:16). The flaming thoughts do not belong to us unless we embrace them.

> "For our struggle is not against flesh and blood, but against the rulers, against the powers, against the world forces of this darkness, against the spiritual forces of wickedness in the heavenly places."
> - Ephesians 6:12

ILLUSTRATION: THE BATTLE FOR THE MIND

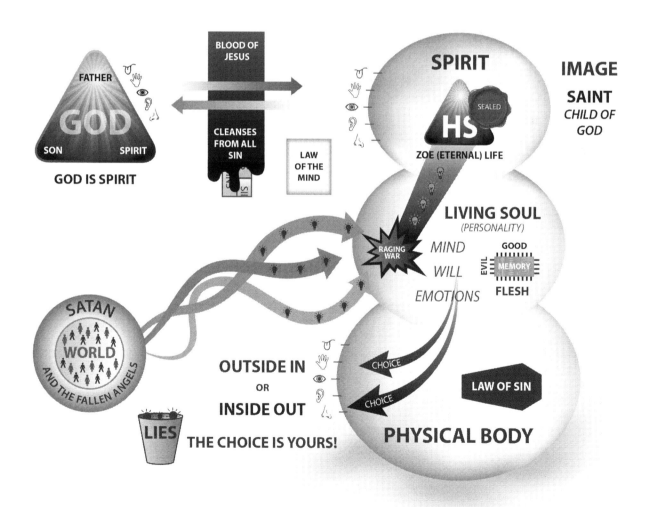

WHAT DOES VICTORY OVER SATAN LOOK LIKE?

1 Corinthians 10:13 tells us that God gives us a successful way out from every temptation we face. Our escape comes when, through Christ, we reject the lie (the temptation), believe the truth of what God says, and then choose to walk in obedience to God's truth (James 1:12; 4:7).

A war between lies and the truth rages within every believer (Rom. 7:23). The battle ends when we make a choice with our will. Every battle ends in either victory or defeat.

The path to our victory begins with knowing and believing the truth of who God is, who we are in Christ (our identity), and that God meets all our needs (John 8:31-32). The path continues with an understanding of the mental strongholds (lies) that comprise our programmed flesh. As we mentally stand firm on God's truth (Matt. 7:24; Col. 3:2) and wear His armor (Christ's life - Eph. 6:10-18), we are able to resist the devil by submitting to God (1 Cor. 10:13; James 4:7).

We fight the devil mentally in the same way Jesus battled him in the desert (Matt. 4:1-11). Instead of embracing every evil, self-serving thought (lie), Jesus took each thought captive (2 Cor. 10:4-6), replacing it with a truthful thought from God (Phil. 4:8). As we set our mind on the truth, the shield of faith (our belief) extinguishes the fires that come from a wavering mind and the pull of the flesh (1 Kin. 18:21; Eph. 6:16; James 1:8). Victory is accomplished when we choose to act under the direction of the Spirit. This choice is walking in the Spirit (Gal. 5:16, 25) and living from the inside out (Session 4). With triumph in hand through Christ (2 Cor. 2:14), Satan and his forces are forced to flee for the next opportune time (Luke 4:13; James 4:7).

ILLUSTRATION: TARGETING LIES WITH THE TRUTH

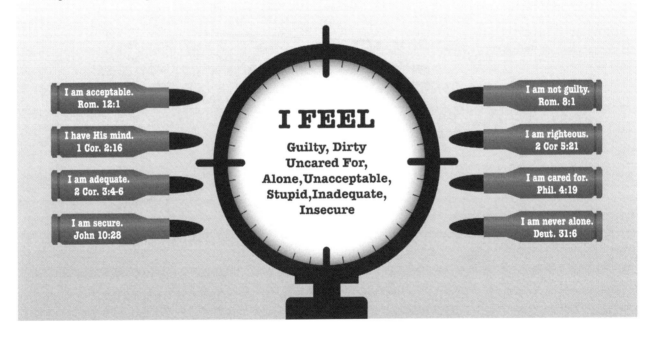

TAKE AIM AT THE LIES. YOUR AMMUNITION IS THE TRUTH.

"For though we walk in the flesh, we do not war according to the flesh, for the weapons of our warfare are not of the flesh, but divinely powerful for the destruction of fortresses. We are destroying speculations and every lofty thing raised up against the knowledge of God, and we are taking every thought captive to the obedience of Christ," 2 Corinthians 10:3-5

I am acceptable. Rom. 12:1

I have His mind. 1 Cor. 2:16

I am adequate. 2 Cor. 3:4-6

I am secure. John 10:28

I FEEL

Guilty, Dirty Uncared For, Alone, Unacceptable, Stupid, Inadequate, Insecure

I am not guilty. Rom. 8:1

I am righteous. 2 Cor 5:21

I am cared for. Phil. 4:19

I am never alone. Deut. 31:6

THE WAY THE MIND WORKS	
We cannot set our mind on two things at once.	Feelings usually follow what our mind is set on.
If we do not set our mind, it will automatically set on something else.	We cannot suppress a thought, but we can replace one thought with another.

WHAT ARE SOME COMMON DECEPTIONS ABOUT VICTORY?

Christians, and many non-Christians, agree on the need to eradicate evil from our lives and the world. Sinful deeds such as murder, rape, and child abuse are rarely embraced, and many methods have been implemented in an attempt to prevent these evils. The world's methods usually involve more laws, more law enforcement, more education, more money, and more (or less) religion. The problem with these paths to victory is they never lead to success. Without God, humanity cannot prevent their dead, depraved hearts from continually leading them to evil (Jer. 17:9; Rom. 3:23).

Many Christians also develop false ideas of how to achieve victory over sin. After accepting Christ by grace through faith, we can be tempted to apply self-discipline and religious performance to uphold God's laws and commands (Gal. 3:1-3). This approach is self-reliance. Self-discipline never leads to our salvation or victory. Control of self comes only from the presence of and reliance on the Holy Spirit (Gal. 5:23).

> "nevertheless knowing that a man is not justified by the works of the Law but through faith in Christ Jesus, even we have believed in Christ Jesus, so that we may be justified by faith in Christ and not by the works of the Law; since by the works of the Law no flesh will be justified." - Galatians 2:16

HOW IS VICTORY CONNECTED TO SPIRITUAL MATURITY?

In Session 13, we saw that God began a maturing work in us that He will complete (Phil. 1:6). The apostle Paul said this transformational growth happens in our mind (Rom. 12:2; Eph. 4:22-24). Jesus said if we remain focused on His teachings, we will know the truth, and the truth will make us free (John 8:31-32). The more we intimately know God and His unconditional love, the more we believe and receive God's provision for our needs. The more we believe who we are in Christ and everything we have received in Him (2 Pet. 1:3), the more we choose to submit our will to His leading and direction (Rom. 12:1). The Spirit's job is to remind us of these truths (John 14:26) (Session 11). He propels us towards this growth and maturity (1 Cor. 3:6), but it takes mental activity on our part (2 Cor. 10:5; 1 Pet. 2:2). Through mental practice, our senses are trained to discern good and evil, resulting in experiencing more victory and maturity (Heb. 5:14).

A WORD OF CAUTION: Even though God's purpose for every believer is growth and maturity, a more mature believer is not more accepted or favored by God. We are accepted by God, not because of our victories, but through Christ's work at the cross (Rom. 8:1, 39; Eph. 2:8). However, God desires for us to walk in the victory He has provided in Christ (1 Cor. 15:57). Our victory is His victory, and our victories bring Him great joy and pleasure (Rom. 8:37; 2 Cor. 5:9).

> "For I am confident of this very thing, that He who began a good work in you will perfect it until the day of Christ Jesus."
> - Philippians 1:6

CAUTION

SUMMARY

Christ secured the victory once and for all at the cross, but He has not yet banished Satan and the forces of evil in this world. God made us new spiritually, but He left us temporarily in our dying bodies with a choice to live either from the inside out or from the outside in. God has not erased our memories, instead He asks and instructs us to consider ourselves dead to the old fleshly ways and alive to His life within us. The war is being waged each and every day in our minds. When we reject the lies, believe the truth, and move under the direction and power of the Holy Spirit, we walk in the victory that is ours in Christ.

TRANSFORM

1. How can I recognize when a thought is a lie from Satan?

    _____

    _____

    _____

    _____

    _____

    _____

    _____

    _____

2. When am I most susceptible to Satan's lies?

    _____

    _____

    _____

    _____

    _____

    _____

    _____

    _____

3. What lies contribute to spiritual defeat in my life?

_____

_____

_____

_____

_____

_____

_____

4. What thoughts or behaviors am I trying to improve through self-effort or religious performance?

_____

_____

_____

_____

_____

_____

_____

_____

_____

5. What examples of victory have I experienced in my Christian life?

_____

_____

_____

_____

_____

_____

_____

_____

_____

6.   Take some time to listen. What is the Holy Spirit telling me in this session?

_____

_____

_____

_____

_____

_____

7.   How will the Holy Spirit's revelation impact my beliefs, choices, and behaviors?

_____

_____

_____

_____

_____

_____

 **PRAY**

Father, You are a wonderful provider. I am engaged in a battle every day in my mind, but You have given me powerful weapons that can tear down any mental stronghold built up against You. Thank You for Your Son, Jesus, who has given me victory over sin and Satan. Thank You for giving me Your truth which exposes the lies that lead to my destruction. Thank You for Your Holy Spirit who is faithful to bring truth to my mind at the right time. May I continually take every thought captive by believing only Your voice and resting in Your provision. I faithfully submit my will to Your will because I know You are love and only have my best interest at heart. Father, thank You for glorifying Yourself in my life today. Amen.

IDENTIFYING OUR FLESH
Exposing the Counterfeit Life

 CONNECT

- What has God revealed to you since we last met?

- Why is it hard to share personal failures and struggles?

- How could a person benefit from reflecting on their personal history?

- What makes a memory painful?

- What makes a memory good?

 RENEW

EXPOSING THE COUNTERFEIT LIFE

In Session 7 we defined and described the flesh and talked about its development. The flesh is the resource we use in an attempt to meet our needs apart from God. If we are designed to contain and express God's life but we choose not to, then we must invent a counterfeit life to obtain meaning, purpose, and provision for our needs. Since all are born dead and separated from God, the programming of our flesh begins from early childhood. In this session, we have an opportunity to ask God to expose our flesh so we can walk more consistently in the victory found in submitting to the Holy Spirit.

WHY WOULD WE WANT TO LOOK AT OUR FLESH PATTERNS?

Examining our flesh patterns may be one of the hardest exercises we will ever do. Looking at one's flesh often involves identifying painful messages and emotions from past experiences. Sharing these memories with others can also lead to fear due to the risks of greater transparency and vulnerability.

Going through the often, painful experience of discovering one's flesh patterns might be compared to a cancer patient visiting the doctor. If the doctor tells the patient that he must operate and cut out the cancer, even if the surgery is extremely painful, the patient realizes that this is the best scenario for his or her cure. And so it is with discovering flesh patterns - although the process is often painful, it can be extremely helpful along the path to experiencing the cure for living in bondage and misery.

However, if we are not walking in the Spirit moment by moment every day, then we are walking after the flesh. We are not living out of Christ's life. We are operating out of our false beliefs. Until we face our false beliefs and replace them with the truth of who we are in Christ, we will continue to walk after our flesh (Prov. 4:18-19; Eph. 5:13-14) (Session 14). We will live in the frustration of Romans 7 and not in the victory of Romans 8.

SPECIFIC REASONS TO LOOK AT OUR FLESH PATTERNS

To expose false identities – By looking at our flesh patterns, we allow God to expose the lies that have led to incorrect self-concepts. Once the lies are exposed, their power is broken as we abide in the truth of our identity in Christ (Session 10).

To expose alternate need-meeters – Our flesh patterns always reveal the objects of our dependence. Once we allow God to expose our idols, we set our minds on God and the fact that He alone meets ALL our needs (Session 3).

To enjoy healthier relationships – Walking after the flesh is the source of chaos and conflict in our relationships. When we allow God to expose our flesh patterns, we discover the personal schemes and traps of our enemy. Once the patterns are exposed, avoiding chaos and conflict becomes easier as we submit to God (Session 14).

To heal from past hurts through forgiveness – Discovering our flesh requires looking back at painful events in our lives. Healing and health come from forgiving each and every person who has offended us. As we become aware of people we have not forgiven, we can choose to release the debt and forgive them (Session 17).

To learn how our emotions connect to our beliefs – The process of discovering our flesh patterns allows us to see the connection between our emotions and our beliefs. Since emotions generally follow what we believe, we can use them as indicators to lead us to the lies we currently accept as truth. Once we replace the lies with truth, emotions usually follow.

FIRST STEP: STAND CONFIDENTLY IN OUR NEW IDENTITY

For a review of our incredible new identity in Christ, see Session 10.

Before we begin to discover our flesh patterns, we must know and believe our new identity in Christ. If we are depending on our performance and not on Christ for our worth and value, we will find it difficult to analyze our behavior and the underlying false beliefs. Instead of seeing the truth and rejecting lies, our energy will be spent downplaying our failures or blaming others for them (Gen. 3:10-13). As we stand on the assurance of God's grace and favor through Christ, we can bring our past actions to His light. We can then see clearly if our behavior is an expression of God or an act of the flesh (John 3:21).

SECOND STEP: FILLING IN OUR OWN FLESH DIAGRAMS

This next section includes a series of worksheets which are a part of an exercise that can be very helpful when done under the direction of the Holy Spirit. Usually, this exercise is more effective to go through with a safe, trusted person who has already worked through these sheets.

HISTORY TAKING SEQUENCE

Ask the Holy Spirit to walk you mentally back through your life history. Focus on significant events that stand out. (See the History Taking Sequence below for potential areas to examine). Then fill out the following worksheet pages.

FAMILY

Birth Order
Siblings
Divorce or Deaths
Financial Status

MOM AND DAD'S RELATIONSHIP

Fights
Who is Dominant?
Affection and Communication

MOTHER / FATHER / CAREGIVER

(start with the most painful relationship)
Attention: Together, Interest in Activities, Communication
Expectations: What Would Please Them?
Absent or Present?
Rejections
Personality
Affection

EARLY YEARS

Describe Yourself
Age 9 and Younger
Trauma and Pain?
3-5 Memories

SCHOOL

Grades: Mom and Dad's Reaction
Social: Loner, Leader, Follower, Many, One

DATING

Broken Hearts
Fears, Rejections
Sexual Issues

WORK

Authority
Job Changes: Fear of Failure

MARRIAGE

Hurts and Rejections
Problems
Divorce

TRAUMAS

Sexual Abuse
Physical Abuse
Verbal Abuse
Abortion

SPIRITUAL HISTORY

Concept of God

		EVENT 1	EVENT 2
AGE	Enter your age at the time.		
PERSON	Person(s) involved		
EVENT	Ask the Holy Spirit to walk you mentally back through your life history. Focus on significant events that stand out. (See the History Taking Sequence on the previous page for potential areas to examine.) As you start to remember certain pleasant or painful memories, record the details here.		
MESSAGES/ BELIEFS	At the moment of the event, what did you believe about yourself? (I.e. "I am loved, accepted" or "I am unloved, rejected" etc. See the included typical belief sheets.)		
FEELINGS	Write out several words (use the Feeling Words Sheet) that describe how you felt at the moment of the event. Get in touch with your emotions.		
BEHAVIORS	Write out how you responded to or coped with the event. (See Manifestations of the Flesh sheets for ideas.)		
TRUTH	Look up scriptures that reinforce the truth of your identity. (See the Aspects of Our Identity sheets in Session 10 to get started.)		

EVENT 3	EVENT 4	EVENT 5	
			AGE
			PERSON
			EVENT
			MESSAGES/ BELIEFS
			FEELINGS
			BEHAVIORS
			TRUTH

	EVENT 6	EVENT 7	EVENT 8
AGE			
PERSON			
EVENT			
MESSAGES/ BELIEFS			
FEELINGS			
BEHAVIORS			
TRUTH			

EVENT 9	EVENT 10	EVENT 11	
			AGE
			PERSON
			EVENT
			MESSAGES/ BELIEFS
			FEELINGS
			BEHAVIORS
			TRUTH

STRENGTH AND ADEQUACY

- I am inadequate.
- I am not strong.
- I am weak.
- I am helpless.
- I don't measure up.
- I am never right.
- I lack faith.
- I am out of control.
- I am useless.

- I am defective. ("Something is wrong with me.")
- I am hopeless.
- I am a loser.
- I am a failure.
- I am stupid.
- I am incompetent.
- I am ugly.

SAFETY AND SECURITY

- I am a fearful / anxious person.
- I am not safe.
- I am insecure.
- I am unprotected.
- I am doomed.
- I am the victim.
- I am exposed.
- I am in bondage.
- I am on the outside.
- I am vulnerable.
- I am lost.
- I am on my own. ("I won't be taken care of.")

TYPICAL NEGATIVE BELIEFS ABOUT OURSELVES

ACCEPTANCE AND BELONGING

- I am not loved.
- I am not accepted.
- I don't belong.
- I am not desirable.
- I am not understood.
- I don't fit in.
- I am not welcome.
- I am not special.
- I am left out.
- I am not interesting.
- I am unwanted.
- I am alone.
- I am awkward.

WORTH AND VALUE

- I am worthless.
- I am not lovable.
- I am not respectable.
- I am not important.
- I am a mistake.
- I am invisible.
- I am not enough.
- I am a nobody.
- I am not special.
- I am disposable.
- I am nothing.
- I am dirty.
- I am not valuable.
- I don't deserve to be loved or cared for.
- I am only as good as what I do.

- I am wrong.
- I am guilty.
- I am broken.
- I am no good.
- I am flawed.
- I am trouble.
- I am crazy.
- I am a bad person.
- I am evil.
- I am damaged (goods).
- I am inferior.
- I am a mess.
- I am cursed.
- I am plain and dull.
- I don't matter.
- I am a disappointment

STRENGTH AND ADEQUACY

- I am adequate.
- I am strong.
- I am powerful.
- I am enough.
- I measure up.
- I am right.
- I am in control.
- I am useful.

- I have what it takes.
- I am hopeful.
- I am a winner.
- I am a success.
- I am smart.
- I am competent.
- I am attractive.
- I am capable.

SAFETY AND SECURITY

- I am untouchable.
- I am invincible.
- I am safe.
- I am secure.
- I am protected.
- I am not a victim.
- I am free.
- I am on the inside.
- I am not vulnerable.
- I am supported.

ACCEPTANCE AND BELONGING

- I am loved.
- I am accepted.
- I belong.
- I am desirable.
- I am understood.
- I fit in.
- I am priviledged
- I am welcome.
- I am special.
- I am included.
- I am interesting.
- I am wanted.

WORTH AND VALUE

- I am valuable.
- I am lovable.
- I am respectable.
- I am important.
- I am number one.
- I am enough.
- I am a somebody.
- I am special.
- I am indispensible.
- I am amazing.
- I am better than most.
- I deserve to be loved or cared for.
- I am right.
- I am not guilty.

- I am good.
- I am perfect.
- I am good luck.
- I am wise.
- I am a good person.
- I am the envy of all my friends.
- I am superior.
- I have everything together.
- I am charming.
- I am exciting.
- I matter.
- I am a overachiever.

FEELING WORDS (PAGE 1)

WORDS EXPRESSING HAPPINESS

I FELT

Alive	Elated	Glad	Optimistic	Relieved	Up
Amused	Energized	Good	Overjoyed	Rested	Warm
Calm	Excited	Great	Peaceful	Satisfied	Wonderful
Cheerful	Fantastic	Hopeful	Pleased	Spirited	
Content	Fortunate	Lively	Proud	Thankful	
Delight	Friendly	Loving	Refreshed	Thrilled	
Ecstatic	Fulfilled	Motherly	Relaxed	Turned on	

WORDS EXPRESSING SADNESS

I FELT

Awful	Desperate	Disturbed	Hurt	Painful	Unloved
Bad	Devastated	Down	Let down	Sorry	Upset
Blue	Disappointed	Embarrassed	Lonely	Terrible	
Bummed out	Discouraged	Gloomy	Lost	Turned off	
Crushed	Dissatisfied	Glum	Low	Uneasy	
Depressed	Distressed	Hopeless	Miserable	Unhappy	

WORDS EXPRESSING ANGER

I FELT

Agitated	Critical	Fed up	Irate	Perturbed	Sore
Aggravated	Disgusted	Frustrated	Irritated	Put out	Ticked off
Annoyed	Dismayed	Furious	Livid	Riled	Uptight
Bitter	Enraged	Hostile	Mad	Resentful	Upset
Burned up	Envious	Impatient	Outraged	Seething	Worked up

WORDS EXPRESSING CONFUSION

I FELT

Anxious	Dazed	Frustrated	Mixed up	Shocked	Trapped
Baffled	Disorganized	Helpless	Mystified	Stuck	Troubled
Bewildered	Disoriented	Hopeless	Paralyzed	Stunned	Uncertain
Bothered	Distracted	Jolted	Perplexed	Surprised	Undecided
Crazy	Disturbed	Lost	Puzzled	Tangled	Unsure

FEELING WORDS (PAGE 2)

WORDS EXPRESSING EMBARRASSMENT

Awkward	Conspicuous	Flustered	Humiliated	Uncomfortable	Shy	
Clumsy	Disgraced	Foolish	Mortified	Shamed	Silly	

I FELT

WORDS EXPRESSING FEAR

Afraid	Chicken	Horrified	Lonely	Tense	Unsure
Anxious	Edgy	Insecure	Nervous	Terrified	Worried
Apprehensive	Fearful	Intimidated	Panicky(ed)	Threatened	
Awed	Frightened	Jittery	Shaky	Timid	
Cautious	Hesitant	Jumpy	Spooked	Uneasy	

I FELT

WORDS EXPRESSING WEAKNESS

Ashamed	Discouraged	Helpless	Inferior	Run-down	Tired
Blocked	Embarrassed	Hopeless	Insecure	Shaky	Unsure
Bored	Exhausted	Horrible	Lifeless	Shy	Useless
Defenseless	Fragile	Ill	Lost	Small	Vulnerable
Demoralized	Frail	Impotent	Overwhelmed	Stressed	Worn out
Disorganized	Frustrated	Inadequate	Powerless	Stupid	Weak
Distracted	Guilty	Incapable	Quiet	Timid	

I FELT

WORDS EXPRESSING STRENGTH

Active	Capable	Happy	Positive	Solid
Aggressive	Confident	Healthy	Potent	Spirited
Alert	Determined	Intense	Powerful	Super
Bold	Eager	Loving	Quick	Sure
Brave	Energetic	Open	Secure	Tough

I FELT

MANIFESTATIONS OF THE FLESH

Manifestations of the Flesh are strategies of living or behavioral coping mechanisms. Below is a list of words and phrases which may portray you much of the time when you are under pressure. As you read through this list, place a check next to any behaviors you have found yourself using.

TO COPE WHEN THINGS AREN'T GOING RIGHT OR GOING MY WAY I TEND TO ...

Withdraw or become emotionally insulated by:

❏ being aloof
❏ acting inhibited
❏ becoming complacent
❏ pulling away
❏ going into a shell
❏ running and hiding
❏ avoiding others
❏ avoiding conflict at all cost
❏ cutting off communication (silent treatment)
❏ keeping people at a distance
❏ bottling up my emotions
❏ avoiding intimacy
❏ becoming a busy body
❏ denying feelings
❏ not expressing feelings and opinions openly and honestly
❏ not expressing love
❏ coming across as:
   ❏ insensitive
   ❏ uncaring
   ❏ indifferent
   ❏ unconcerned
   ❏ unsympathetic
❏ ignoring problems and hoping they'll go away
❏ denying anything is wrong or bad
❏ lying
❏ deceiving others and myself
❏ exaggerating
❏ fantasizing
❏ playing games to hide my real intentions

Perform for acceptance by:

❏ trying to be all things to all people
❏ doing the "proper or correct" thing
❏ keeping everyone happy at any cost
❏ avoiding any conflict

❏ becoming a doormat (letting others take advantage of me)
❏ telling others what I think they want to hear
❏ giving in to others too easily
❏ being overly apologetic
❏ allowing others to control me
❏ acting pretentious - (phony, unreal)
❏ becoming superficial (plastic)
❏ focusing on appearing good to others
❏ being gushy (too sentimental)
❏ having difficulty saying no
❏ not setting boundaries
❏ not standing up for myself
❏ becoming obsessed with:
   ❏ accomplishments
   ❏ recognition
   ❏ status
   ❏ how I look
   ❏ what others think of me
   ❏ my physical health
❏ devotion to a cause, structure, order, rules, regulations
❏ faking it (hiding what I feel)
❏ putting on a show to get attention

Resort to passivity by:

❏ quitting too easily
❏ not taking chances
❏ playing it safe
❏ waiting for someone to tell me what to do and how to think
❏ depending on others instead of God
❏ vacillating
❏ becoming indecisive
❏ wanting someone else to make the decision
❏ avoiding failure at all cost
❏ procrastinating
❏ being irresponsible
❏ being lazy, apathetic, lethargic

Become too intense by:

❏ becoming stoical (unemotional)
❏ being overly analytical
❏ being stern (solemn/formal)
❏ lacking joy or life
❏ not being fun to be with

Embrace anxiousness and tension by:

❏ fearing the worst
❏ becoming paralyzed
❏ creating endless "what if" scenarios
❏ being overly suspicious (paranoid)
❏ acting restless (high strung)
❏ losing patience
❏ finding it hard to relax
❏ experiencing stress related illnesses
❏ looking for strength or guidance in divination:
  ❏ horoscopes
  ❏ fortune telling
  ❏ tarot cards
  ❏ palm reading
  ❏ ouija boards
  ❏ and/or the occult

Escape pain/pressure and become self-indulgent by:

❏ being impulsive (lacking self control)
❏ buying things to feel better
❏ assuming "if it feels good, do it"
❏ overeating
❏ developing addictions to:
  ❏ alcohol
  ❏ drugs
  ❏ cigarettes
  ❏ caffeine
  ❏ sex, fantasy
  ❏ pornography
  ❏ partying
  ❏ television, movies, entertainment
  ❏ technology
  ❏ religion and religious activity
  ❏ sleeping
  ❏ work, career, business, job, school
  ❏ talking or texting
  ❏ sugar
  ❏ junk food
  ❏ the internet, social media
  ❏ hobbies
  ❏ games
  ❏ reading
  ❏ other _____

Try to dominate or control others by:

❏ acting dictatorial (bossy)
❏ being demanding (pushy)
❏ being overbearing (controlling)
❏ manipulating
❏ intimidating
❏ being uncooperative (unteachable)
❏ arguing
❏ being rigid and non-flexible
❏ being closed-minded
❏ being stubborn
❏ being obstinate
❏ being unreasonable
❏ being unyielding
❏ overprotecting
❏ being possessive (selfish)
❏ preaching (lecturing)
❏ becoming overly responsible
❏ making decisions for others
❏ giving unsolicited advice
❏ trying to prevent other's failures
❏ trying to find someone who needs me and who I can rescue
❏ nagging
❏ talking too much and listening poorly
❏ demanding my rights
❏ blackmailing (making threats)
❏ resisting authority
❏ causing dissension (strife)
❏ irritating others (aggravating)
❏ using profanity
❏ giving the silent treatment
❏ being moody
❏ using guilt
❏ giving gifts with strings attached
❏ showing favoritism
❏ engaging in passive/aggressive behavior
❏ playing tricks and using deception
❏ throwing fits

more on the next page . . .

Become hostile to myself by:

❏ harboring bitterness
❏ keeping a scorecard of wrongs done to me
❏ stuffing my anger and frustrations
❏ cutting myself
❏ starving myself (anorexia)
❏ binging and purging (bulimia)
❏ focusing on my suffering and trials to get
    attention and sympathy
❏ playing the role of a victim/martyr
❏ mentally punishing myself
❏ being self depreciating
❏ being too hard on myself
❏ being hypersensitive to criticism
❏ being uncomfortable with success
❏ assuming I am always the problem
❏ condemning myself for mistakes
❏ taking things too personally
❏ reading in rejection when it isn't there
❏ setting things up to bring about rejections
❏ engaging in self-pity
❏ having difficulty receiving love
❏ having difficulty receiving compliments
❏ not receiving other's forgiveness
❏ not forgiving myself

Display self-righteousness and judgmentalism by:

❏ depending on myself instead of God
❏ becoming proud and arrogant
❏ being egocentric
❏ bragging
❏ acting conceited
❏ becoming defensive
❏ having a superior attitude
❏ pretending to know it all
❏ not asking for help
❏ making excuses
❏ covering up and hiding mistakes
❏ pointing to someone or something else as the
    problem (blaming)
❏ not taking responsibility for failure or problems
❏ being critical of others
❏ not admitting I was wrong
❏ being slow to apologize
❏ having difficulty asking forgiveness

❏ not expressing gratitude
❏ constantly dwelling on the faults of others
❏ nit-picking things to death
❏ becoming prejudiced (intolerant)
❏ complaining (being negative)

Become hostile to others by:

❏ being unfriendly
❏ picking fights
❏ speaking harshly
❏ bullying
❏ being sarcastic
❏ spreading rumors
❏ gossiping
❏ using put-downs
❏ making fun of others
❏ having a quick temper
❏ slandering
❏ seeking to get even
❏ yelling and screaming
❏ using threats
❏ becoming physically abusive
❏ desiring others to fail or get hurt
❏ being easily irritated (touchy)

TRANSFORM

1. As I record different events on my diagram, what feelings regularly surface?

    _____

    _____

    _____

    _____

    _____

2. As I record different events on my diagram, what false beliefs repeat?

    _____

    _____

    _____

    _____

    _____

3. How do my flesh patterns impact my relationships with others today?

    _____

    _____

    _____

    _____

    _____

    _____

4. How will understanding my flesh patterns help me embrace the truth?

    _____

    _____

    _____

    _____

    _____

PRAY

Father, thank You for making me new and giving me Your life. Thank You for starting Your work in me with the gift of righteousness and a new identity. Thank You for continuing to complete the work of aligning my behavior with my new identity. Thank You for Your forgiveness and freedom from condemnation which allow me to look objectively at my sins and any false beliefs about You or myself I continue to hold. Thank You for Your Spirit who leads me into all truth and for Your kindness which leads me to repentance. As You reveal to me any areas where I am trusting in others or myself to find meaning or purpose in life, I desire to believe the truth and choose to walk in Your life, peace, and victory. Thank You for revealing to me any flesh patterns preventing the enjoyment and display of Your life. You alone satisfy my soul. Amen.

16

BROKENNESS AND SURRENDER
Unveiling Life

CONNECT

- What has God revealed to you since we last met?

- Why does God allow suffering and pain in your life?

- How do you handle suffering and pain in your life?

- Think of an instance of significant personal suffering. What do you believe God was doing in that time?

RENEW

BURDENS, TEMPTATIONS, AND OUR ABILITIES

What is a burden? A burden is something out of our control that is difficult or hard. Burdens weigh us down physically, mentally, and/or emotionally. We can bring burdens upon ourselves by choosing to walk after the flesh (sinning) (Gal. 6:7-8). Sin often brings with it unpleasant and overwhelming consequences. Outside forces can also place burdens on us. These imposed burdens include job loss, family betrayal or infidelity, illness, the death of a loved one, disabilities, natural disasters, etc.

Burdens are not the same as temptations. Temptations are mental attacks from Satan, who uses the world and our flesh to distract us from believing God's truths and living out of His life. According to 1 Corinthians 10:13, God will not allow us to experience a temptation we cannot bear (escape from). With burdens, God gives us no such promise. Instead, Jesus promises we will have trouble (John 16:33). He even allows burdens beyond our ability to bear (2 Cor. 1:8-9).

". . . God is faithful, who will not allow you to be tempted beyond what you are able, but with the temptation will provide the way of escape also, so that you will be able to endure it."
- 1 Corinthians 10:13

ILLUSTRATION: DIFFERENCE BETWEEN TEMPTATIONS AND BURDENS

TEMPTATIONS

Temptations are spiritual attacks we can control in Christ. God empowers believers with the Holy Spirit to provide a way of escape so that we can experience His faithfulness (1 Cor. 10:13) (Session 14).

DIFFERENT THAN

SPIRIT

HS

ZOE (ETERNAL) LIFE

LIVING SOUL
(PERSONALITY)

MIND
WILL
EMOTIONS

GOOD
MEMORY
EVIL
Flesh

PHYSICAL BODY

SATAN
WORLD
AND THE FALLEN ANGELS

BURDENS

Burdens are difficult events we cannot control. God uses burdens to show us that our programmed flesh is broken and teach us to trust in HIM to meet our needs (2 Cor. 1:8-9).

ABUSE
PAIN
GRIEFS
ABANDONMENT
DIVORCE
SICKNESS
CARES
REJECTION
BETRAYAL
ADULTERY

"For we do not want you to be unaware, brethren, of our affliction which came to us in Asia, that we were burdened excessively, beyond our strength, so that we despaired even of life; indeed, we had the sentence of death within ourselves so that we would not trust in ourselves, but in God who raises the dead;"
- 2 Corinthians 1:8-9

BURDENS BRING SUFFERING

Suffering is the pain we experience from the loss of something we value. What type of suffering do burdens bring? Suffering can take many forms – spiritual (oppression from demons), mental anguish (worry, anxiety, hyper-active mind), emotional (depression, fear, anger), and physical (high blood pressure, headaches). The degree of mental and emotional suffering is determined by the value we place on what is lost, damaged, or destroyed.

PURPOSE OF BURDENS AND SUFFERING

God's purpose for humanity, as discussed in Session 4, is to glorify Him (which means to manifest, display, or express His life). How then does He work in the midst of burdens and suffering to achieve this over-arching purpose? God uses burdens in our lives to take us beyond our own resources so we will grow in dependence on Him (2 Pet. 3:18). This dependence provides an opportunity for greater intimacy with Him. As we experience this intimacy, the display of His life/light/love becomes increasingly evident and brings glory to Him (Is. 48:10; John 9:1-3; 2 Cor. 4:6-10; 1 Pet. 1:6-7).

SUFFERING THAT LEADS TO BROKENNESS

What are the possible responses to suffering (Acts 7:51; 2 Cor. 12:9)? Because suffering is painful and difficult, one response is anger towards the person who brought the suffering. God can also become the object of our anger since He is all-powerful and able to prevent suffering. Anger, nursed through constant mental reinforcement, becomes bitterness.

God desires a different response – one of brokenness and surrender (Ps. 51:17; 1 Pet. 5:6-7). Brokenness is the conclusion that our resources are completely bankrupt and inadequate to meet our needs and provide the abundant life He designed for us (Jer. 2:5; Matt. 5:3). Believers who are experiencing brokenness do not have a dysfunctional nature. Rather, they are coming to the conclusion that the "flesh profits nothing" (John 6:63) and apart from Christ, they can do nothing (John 15:5).

When we respond with brokenness and surrender, we more fully display the life of God which indwells us. When we trust God's love and power, we lean into His purposes and timing (Prov. 3:5-6; Jer. 29:11-13; Rom. 5:3-4; James 1:2-5). When we come to Him with our burdens, we can gain His perspective on our situation (2 Cor. 1:8-9; 3:4-5; 12:7-10; 1 Pet. 5:5). He opens our eyes to those things we overvalue. As God reveals to us those counterfeit need-meeters, He additionally exposes our flesh patterns and the lies we believe about ourselves, about Him, and about others. God wants to use burdens and resulting suffering to open our eyes to the bankruptcy of using anything other than Him to meet our needs (Heb. 12:5-11). Our methods of meeting needs from our own resources conflict with what God wishes to do in and through us (Gal. 5:16-21; Phil. 3:3).

"And He has said to me, 'My grace is sufficient for you, for power is perfected in weakness.' Most gladly, therefore, I will rather boast about my weaknesses, that the power of Christ may dwell in me."
- 2 Corinthians 12:9

SURRENDERING RIGHTS

What is a "right?" By definition it is something we are owed or deserve. In the context of this session, a right is something we perceive as an entitlement. Our perceived rights usually pertain to our needs. When one of our rights is withheld, violated, or unattainable, we experience frustration, anxiety, anger, disappointment, and/or desperation. Examples of rights people hold tightly include: the right to have a good income, a good home, or a good reputation; the right to be understood, loved, respected, or married; or the right to have a spouse who responds to us as we think appropriate.

God leads us to surrender all our rights to Him. His path to freedom and joy in the Spirit is experienced through laying down these rights (Matt. 16:25; John 3:26-30). As we surrender our rights, we agree with God that HE is our life (Ps. 36:9; Matt. 10:39; 2 Cor. 4:11; Col. 3:4a). He is sufficient to meet ALL our needs (Phil. 4:19), and He will determine the outcomes of the situation according to HIS will, not our expectations (Prov. 16:33). Through surrender, we acknowledge to God that He is sufficient, and we are not.

"who, although He existed in the form of God, did not regard equality with God a thing to be grasped, but emptied Himself, taking the form of a bond-servant,"
- Philippians 2:6-7

God asks us to take the same path of surrender that Jesus went through on His way to the cross.

"And He withdrew from them about a stone's throw, and He knelt down and began to pray, saying, 'Father, if You are willing, remove this cup from Me; yet not My will, but Yours be done.'" - Luke 22:41-42

We allow Him to accomplish what He wills (Phil. 1:6) and to make something beautiful of our lives, even more incredible than what we can imagine (Eccl. 3:11; Is. 61:3; Rom. 8:28-29; 1 Pet. 5:10).

Jesus is our perfect example of how to surrender rights. He began His journey to "fulfill all righteousness" and complete the work on the cross by first surrendering His rights. In Philippians 2:5-8, we read that Jesus "emptied Himself," giving up every right He had as God. What were some of the rights He surrendered? What were the results? Jesus surrendered everything to the Father including His right to life (Luke 22:42). The Father honored that complete surrender, and through Jesus, He birthed millions of new believers who can, in turn, display the life of God through their own brokenness and surrender (2 Cor. 4:7-11; 5:14-15; Heb. 2:9-10). Jesus is not just an example for us to try to imitate. He is an example of us (Rom. 8:29; 1 John 4:17b).

SUMMARY

God uses burdens in our lives to bring about brokenness. In the midst of suffering He often reveals counterfeit need-meeters and our futile strategies of dependence on our own resources. God leads us to surrender our rights, allowing us to experience His abundant supply. As we surrender rights, we experience the love, joy, and peace found in Christ's life.

TRANSFORM

1. What burdens and suffering have I experienced?

_____

_____

_____

_____

_____

2. In what ways have my burdens and suffering led me to greater dependence on God?

_____

_____

_____

_____

_____

3. In what ways have I continued to rely on the flesh despite my burdens and suffering?

_____

_____

_____

_____

_____

_____

4. What keeps me from surrendering my rights?

_____

_____

_____

_____

_____

_____

5. What specific rights (perceived entitlements) have I not surrendered to God? (Ask the Holy Spirit to reveal them to you. Below are some possibilities.)

- My right to possessions
- My right to a good reputation
- My right to be accepted
- My right to be successful
- My right to have pleasant circumstances
- My right to presume on the will of God
- My right to life itself
- My right to beauty or strength
- My right to have friendships
- My right to be heard
- My right to take up offense

- My right to avoid reaping what I sow
- My right to be right
- My right to see results
- My right to be loved by others
- My right to_____
- My right to_____
- My right to_____
- My right to_____
- My right to_____
- My right to_____
- My right to_____

PRAY

Father, I am confident of this very thing that You, who began a good work in me, will perfect it until the day of Christ Jesus. I surrender to You my will, my mind, my emotions, my body, my future plans, my hopes, and my dreams. I give You my home, my marriage, my spouse, my children, my geographical location, my recreation, my entertainment, and my career. I surrender to You my past successes and my past failures, my habits, my finances, my problems, my time, my business conduct and relationships, my Christian walk, and my response to authority. Specifically, I surrender to You the following "rights"

_____

_____

(use list from the Transform question #5)

Because I know You love me and want my best, I give You permission to do anything You wish to me, with me, in me and through me. I once claimed the above items as mine, but now they all belong to You and are under Your control. You can do anything You please with them. I willingly make this commitment in the name and authority of the Lord Jesus Christ, and I recognize that this is an agreement with You that can never be broken. Now that I have surrendered ownership of my life, You will never give it back to me. Amen.

_____

Signed   *Date*

* If the Spirit has led you to surrender your rights to Him today, consider signing this surrender prayer as a way to remember your decision. Satan will tempt you to take back what you have surrendered. Use this as a reminder of the freedom you have chosen through surrendering your rights to God.

17

GIVING AND ASKING FORGIVENESS
Releasing Life

CONNECT

- What has God revealed to you since we last met?

- How do you respond when somebody hurts or offends you?

- What happens to a relationship when there is a hurt or offense?

- In what ways do people reconcile with each other?

RENEW

GIVING FORGIVENESS

What happens to us when we experience rejection? God designed everyone with the need for acceptance, but only He can meet the need for full, unconditional acceptance (Session 3). God also designed us to live in healthy relationships characterized by love (Eph. 4:2). In this fallen world, however, people reject and offend one another. When others reject us, we may feel hurt, and hurt can quickly lead to anger. If we embrace anger as the pathway to manage the hurt, we nurse it until it becomes bitterness (Ps. 73:21-22). This choice can express itself in hostility or the "deeds of the flesh" (Gal. 5:19-21a) which become the programmed flesh patterns we develop to cope with unmet needs for acceptance and worth apart from God (Session 7). These fleshly deeds offend and provoke others around us, which, in turn, provide opportunities for them to feel hurt, become angry, get bitter, and continue the cycle of rejection and hurt. On this bitter path, we no longer walk in the Spirit or experience God's grace (Heb. 12:15).

"BE ANGRY, AND yet DO NOT SIN; do not let the sun go down on your anger, and do not give the devil an opportunity."
- Ephesians 4:26-27

"So, as those who have been chosen of God, holy and beloved, put on a heart of compassion, kindness, humility, gentleness and patience; bearing with one another, and forgiving each other, whoever has a complaint against anyone; just as the Lord forgave you, so also should you."
- Colossians 3:12-13

WHAT DOES GOD WANT US TO DO IF WE EXPERIENCE HURT AND ANGER?

God provided a way for us in Christ to escape the cycle of anger that leads to bitterness and fleshly actions. Instead of holding onto the hurt and anger, we can choose to release them. This decision is called forgiveness, and it is a choice we make to release our offender of any debt we think we are owed. To release and let go means to surrender the offense (including the hurt and anger - Eph. 4:31-32; Col. 3:8) to God and entrust that He will handle the offense in His wisdom, justice, and righteousness (Gen. 18:25; Prov. 20:22; Rom. 12:19; James 4:12). If we continue to bring up the offense, it will serve as a signal that we have not yet released it to God.

While we desire the acceptance of others, our worth and value come from God's acceptance. As we realize God has supplied everything we need (2 Pet. 1:3), the Holy Spirit empowers us to release the rejection (the debt). As we let go of the debt, hurt, and anger, we release life – allowing the expression of Christ's life through us (Luke 23:34). We now see the other person through God's eyes and accept him or her unconditionally (Rom. 15:7).

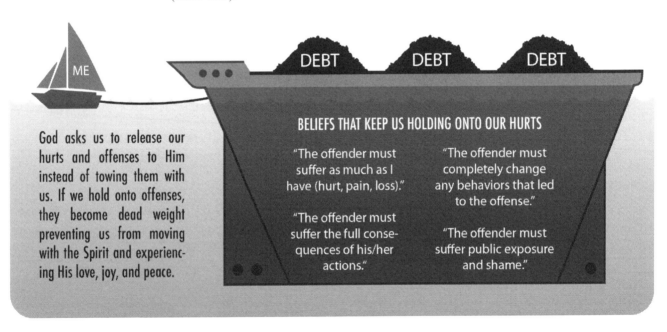

God asks us to release our hurts and offenses to Him instead of towing them with us. If we hold onto offenses, they become dead weight preventing us from moving with the Spirit and experiencing His love, joy, and peace.

BELIEFS THAT KEEP US HOLDING ONTO OUR HURTS

"The offender must suffer as much as I have (hurt, pain, loss)."

"The offender must suffer the full consequences of his/her actions."

"The offender must completely change any behaviors that led to the offense."

"The offender must suffer public exposure and shame."

WHAT ENABLES US TO FORGIVE?

God has forgiven believers completely and unconditionally through Jesus Christ. As we believe and receive His forgiveness, we can freely forgive others and ourselves as we have been forgiven (Col. 2:13-14; 3:13).

Our ability and motivation to forgive only comes from God's life, image, and power within us. God's life is love, and love forgives (Ps. 86:5; Dan. 9:9; 1 Cor. 13:5; 1 John 4:8). The choice to extend forgiveness is not based on how we feel, but on who we are. As new creations, it is our nature (most natural inclination) to forgive. To do otherwise is to walk after the flesh, which is uncharacteristic of our nature (James 1:22-25). When Paul tells us to "forgive one another as Christ has forgiven you" (Eph. 4:32), he is not telling us to try to emulate Jesus' behavior. Jesus forgave out of the Father's life in Him and His true nature. Our ability to forgive unconditionally is based on the same source and nature (John 15:5; 2 Cor. 5:14-15; 1 John 4:7-9).

HOW DO WE FORGIVE ANOTHER?

As the Holy Spirit leads, our path to forgiveness will be unique to our journey. Here is one path to consider:

1. **Acknowledge the hurt.** Charge the debt by acknowledging to God and yourself that it happened. Name the event. Until we acknowledge the hurt, there is nothing to forgive (Ps. 142).

2. **Acknowledge how it made you feel.** Charge the emotional debt by describing to yourself the hurt you felt/feel and the message (belief) that you received as a result of what that person did to you (Ps. 6:6-7).

3. **Release the person from the debt they owe you.** Choose to give the debt to God. Reckon the account settled. Commit to the fact that they never have to make it up to you or pay you back (Rom. 12:19).

4. **Accept the person unconditionally.** Surrender the right for them to change or make you feel loved and accepted. Christ will meet your need for security, love, acceptance, and significance (Rom. 15:7).

5. **Be willing to go forward** in the relationship as if the forgiven offense had not occurred (1 Thess. 5:15; 1 Pet. 3:9). If the relationship is toxic, healthy boundaries are needed. Physical or sexual abuse should never be allowed to continue.

The indwelling Spirit empowers us to forgive others immediately and continuously. As we "pray without ceasing" (1 Thess. 5:17), we can give each offense to the Father, even in the moment the offense occurs.

If we walk after the flesh and choose to embrace anger and cultivate bitterness, we are quenching the Holy Spirit and will not experience His love, joy, and peace (Eph. 4:30). At the moment we recognize we are holding on to offenses, we can immediately thank God for the forgiveness we have in Christ, admit to Him our choice to walk after the flesh, and choose to release the debt (and hurt and anger). An exercise at the end of this session will give us the opportunity to explore the possibility that we have not forgiven some people who have hurt us in our past.

WHAT ARE SOME MISCONCEPTIONS ABOUT FORGIVING?

People hold many misconceptions about what forgiveness is and what it requires of a person. Here are some common beliefs about forgiveness that are NOT Biblical.

1. Forgiveness requires that I no longer feel angry.

"To be a Christian means to forgive the inexcusable because God has forgiven the inexcusable in you."
- C.S. Lewis

"Forgiveness is an act of the will, and the will can function regardless of the temperature of the heart."
- Corrie ten Boom

"When you release the wrongdoer from the wrong, you cut a malignant tumor out of your inner life. You set a prisoner free, but you discover that the real prisoner was yourself."
- Lewis Smedes

> "Forgiveness is not an occasional act, it is a constant attitude."
> - Martin Luther King Jr.

2. The passage of time or the process of forgetting leads to forgiveness.

3. Saying "Let's just forget about it" or denying I have really been hurt; believing forgiveness is pretending the hurt was really not that bad.

4. Forgiveness is justifying, understanding, or explaining away someone's rejecting behavior.

5. Forgiveness means I must tell the offender/s I forgive them.

ASKING FORGIVENESS

> "If therefore you are presenting your offering at the altar, and there remember that your brother has something against you, leave your offering there before the altar, and go your way; first be reconciled to your brother, and then come and present your offering."
> - Matthew 5:23-24

When we hurt someone, the Holy Spirit convinces us of our hurtful action. Acknowledging the wrong, we can choose to confess our action to God and thank Him for the complete forgiveness we received at salvation.

God's heart is for reconciliation, and He desires for us to initiate reconciliation with the person(s) we hurt (Matt. 5:23-24; Rom. 12:18; 14:19). Consequently, our new nature seeks peace and honors others in love (2 Cor. 5:17-18; Eph. 4:29). Reaching out to the offended person indicates we want the relationship restored. It shows that we realize we have done something wrong and are willing to take responsibility.

HINDRANCES TO ASKING FORGIVENESS

When we hurt someone, our enemy (Satan) does not want us to take any steps toward repentance or reconciliation (John 10:10a). Satan sends his fiery darts, or lies, to hinder us from living out of Christ's life, and repairing relationships (Session 14). Here are some examples of hindrances to asking forgiveness.

- **Believing it is not worth the effort** – Consider the alternative. Not apologizing may cost us significantly (emotionally and physically) (Matt. 5:23).

- **Believing it was the other person's fault** – This perspective is justifying our position. As believers, the Spirit leads us to take ownership of our part in the conflict, no matter how small (Phil. 2:3-4; 3:9).

- **Believing that asking forgiveness is a sign of weakness.** – An incorrect belief about our identity can lead to an effort to protect our self from any show of weakness. Our true identity is one of strength and adequacy in Christ (2 Cor. 3:5; 9:8; 12:9).

- **Fear of the other person taking advantage of us** – We cannot control what others do and must let God work in the heart of the other person (Matt. 10:28; Rom. 8:31; Eph. 5:21).

- **The need to be right** – Why must we be right in this situation? What false belief about our identity needs to be addressed? Our worth and value are not based on being right or wrong. Our value comes from God (1 Cor. 1:29-31; 13:5).

- **Pride** – Arrogance is an attitude of superiority (1 Cor. 4:7). Love acts in the best interest of others, whereas, arrogance acts in the best interest of self (1 Cor. 13:4). Asking forgiveness requires us to humble ourselves and submit to the Holy Spirit's leading (James 4:6; 1 Pet. 5:5-6).

- **Fear of losing control** – What if we lose control of the outcome or the future of this relationship? God is in control (Gen. 50:20; Rom. 8:28).

- **Fear of rejection** – What if we are rejected for doing what God asks us to do? Although it may hurt, we can rest in the fact that we are fully accepted by God in Christ (Ps. 94:14; Rom. 8:31) (Session 10).

- **Fear of failure** – An apology is an admission of failure, but we are free to fail because our identity is not based on performance. God loves us unconditionally and has forgiven us all our sins (Phil. 4:13; 1 John 4:18).

- **Believing old offenses do not need to be dealt with now** – God may lead you to ask forgiveness of a person you offended long ago. As we walk in the Spirit, we will follow His direction (Gal. 5:16; Heb. 12:14a).

"God is opposed to the proud, but gives grace to the humble." - James 4:6b

HOW DO WE ASK FORGIVENESS?

As the Holy Spirit leads (when, where, how), our path to asking forgiveness will be unique to our journey. Here is one path to consider:

1. Before going to the person, check your motive (Prov. 16:2; James 4:3). Are you responding to the Holy Spirit or trying to meet a need (acceptance, respect, love, etc.)?

2. Accept responsibility (2 Sam. 12:13; Gal. 6:4-5).

3. Name the offense (James 5:16).

4. Express sorrow and regret (2 Cor. 7:9).

5. Ask for forgiveness (Rom. 12:18; 14:19). This appeal encourages closure to the offense and promotes peace.

6. Discuss what it would take to reconcile the relationship (Luke 19:8).

As the Holy Spirit leads you, here is a simple, short statement to consider using:

"I was wrong when I _____(name specific offense)_____, and I know it hurt you."

"I am sorry." "Will you forgive me?"

"What can I do to make this right?" or "What can I do to reconcile our relationship?"

"If possible, so far as it depends on you, be at peace with all men."
- Romans 12:18

WHAT IF THEY DO NOT FORGIVE US?

We have followed the leading of the Holy Spirit and asked for forgiveness. It is now up to the other person to make the decision to forgive. We cannot control them or heal their hurts. Only God can heal (Ps. 147:3; Is. 53:5; 1 Pet. 2:24). Any further attempts to control or pacify may be an attempt of our flesh to fix something on our own. As the Spirit leads, we pray for the other person and rest, trusting in God to heal the relationship (1 Tim. 2:1; James 5:16b). God is working in each of our lives to bring us both into greater dependence on Him.

If the other person brings up the offense again, we can sincerely ask for forgiveness again. As we ask God to reveal the obstacles to forgiveness, we can be open to exploring together a way to reconcile (James 1:5; 3:17).

DOES FORGIVENESS ALWAYS LEAD TO RECONCILIATION?

In a relationship between two people, both are affected when one hurts or offends the other. Both have a part in the reconciliation (Rom. 12:18; 14:19). The offended must forgive, and the offender must take responsibility for the hurt (offense) in order to restore a healthy relationship. Reconciliation is only possible when both people are willing. Even if the other person is unwilling, a believer can still choose to experience Christ's life and express His life to others.

SUMMARY

If we walk after the flesh, we will hurt and offend each other. God's full forgiveness and our new nature in Christ enable us to forgive. We can choose to forgive the offender by releasing the debt owed and letting go of the hurt and anger. When we offend another, we can seek forgiveness by taking responsibility for our action and asking for forgiveness. We can choose to surrender to the Holy Spirit and express Christ's life through forgiveness, whether a relationship is reconciled or not.

 **PRAY**

Father, thank You for unconditionally forgiving ALL of my sins. Thank You for making me a forgiver in my new nature as Your child. When others hurt me, remind me of who I am - fully accepted by You and complete in my inner being. I desire to always see others through Your eyes, loving and forgiving them unconditionally. When I hurt others, thank You for gently reminding me that I have been walking after the flesh and not looking to You for love and acceptance. Thank You for leading me to pursue forgiveness and reconciliation. Thank You that I have all the love, kindness, and grace I need to live in healthy relationships with others. Amen.

TRANSFORM

FORGIVING PEOPLE WHO HAVE HURT ME IN THE PAST

On the back of this paper, and on a separate sheet if necessary, make a list of all the people in your life (whoever God brings to mind) who have offended or hurt you. You may need to include yourself in this list. Next to each name, note the actual event that happened. Write down the feelings you experienced (e.g. hurt, shame, embarrassment, rejection, abandonment, betrayal, etc.) and the message you received about yourself from that offense in the "How It Affected Me" box. Then choose to forgive the person. A suggested way to process this time of forgiveness is by using the "Empty Chair Exercise."

EMPTY CHAIR EXERCISE

1. With your list in hand, place an empty chair in front of you. For the purpose of this exercise, imagine the person who has offended you actually sitting in the chair.

2. Call the person's name and tell them specifically what they did to hurt you (actual offense).

3. Tell the person the message (feeling/belief) that you received as a result of what they did to you.

4. Now forgive the person, releasing the debt you believe they owe.

   "I forgive you, _____(Their Name)_____. The debt is canceled – paid in full – satisfied by Christ at the cross, and you owe me nothing further." (Avoid saying "I want to forgive you… " or "I would like to forgive you…", etc.)

5. Release to God your right to have them change.

   "Heavenly Father, I surrender my right to see _____(Their Name)_____ change to meet my felt needs. The Lord will supply all my needs according to His riches in glory in Christ Jesus."

6. Now receive the person unconditionally and say to the person in the chair: "I now receive and accept you as you are. I accept the part you have played in bringing me to brokenness and intimacy with my heavenly Father."

After you have forgiven every person on your list, demonstrate that the debt has been canceled by tearing out and destroying all used pages.

FORGIVING PEOPLE WHO HAVE HURT ME IN THE PAST

This page is designed to be used with the forgiveness exercise as described on the previous page.

NAME	EVENT	HOW IT AFFECTED ME

IF YOU NEED MORE SPACE, PLEASE USE THE BLANK SHEET AT THE END OF THIS CHAPTER.

ASKING FORGIVENESS OF PEOPLE I HAVE HURT IN THE PAST

Ask God to reveal any person whom you have offended and have never asked for their forgiveness. Make a list below and continue on a separate paper if necessary. Ask the Holy Spirit for wisdom as to how you should ask forgiveness (timing, place, communication method, words, etc.). Be obedient to His leading, as you rely on His strength, courage, and love.

PERSON I OFFENDED	HOW I OFFENDED THEM	WHEN WILL I ASK FORGIVENESS?

IF YOU NEED MORE SPACE, PLEASE USE THE BACK OF THIS PAPER.

LAW VS. GRACE
Bondage vs. Life

CONNECT

- What has God revealed to you since we last met?

- What was the purpose of God's Law?

- What does it mean to live under laws?

- What is the role of God's grace?

- How did Jesus demonstrate God's grace?

RENEW

WHAT IS LAW?

The Old Covenant Law is a system of demands God placed on Israel's performance (or behavior). Along with the demands, God set up blessings for those Israelites who fulfilled His requirements and curses for those who did not (Ex. 19:3-5, 7-8; Deut. 11:26-32; 28:1-2, 15). God's Law was given to the Israelites so they could know how to represent God to the nations. It served as a guide to train them in righteousness (Gal. 3:24) and to reveal sin (Rom. 7:7). The Law acted as a guardian or manager until Christ fulfilled its purpose (Gal. 3:23; 4:2).

This Law system was recorded at Mt. Sinai, but its roots go all the way back to the Garden of Eden when God told Adam not to eat from the tree of the knowledge of good and evil (Gen. 2:17). As Adam chose to either obey or disobey, he faced the consequences of his actions for good or bad.

"For as many as are of the works of the Law are under a curse; for it is written, 'CURSED IS EVERYONE WHO DOES NOT ABIDE BY ALL THINGS WRITTEN IN THE BOOK OF THE LAW, TO PERFORM THEM.'"
- Galatians 3:10

A system of law-based behavior uses rules, statutes, ordinances, principles, and precepts to guide the choices and behaviors of those under its jurisdiction. A person under this system believes they can achieve right standing with God by following its guidelines. It is a conditional, achieving system based on performance.

WHAT ARE LIMITATIONS OF GOD'S LAW?

God's Law is good and perfect (Rom. 7:12), but what happens when we attempt to live by the Laws of God? The Law shows us the right way to live but does not provide the power to obey (Heb. 8:7; 10:1-2). Instead, the Law appeals to our flesh, igniting sinful passions (Rom. 7:5). Law is to sinful desire as oxygen is to fire (1 Cor. 15:56).

Law also increases sin (Rom. 5:20a). The more Law we use to direct or manage our behavior, the more we will find ourselves sinning (Rom. 7:8-9).

The word "sin" means to miss the mark. God's Law is His standard which defines the "mark." The Law is a set of standards that give a reference point but does not impart life (Gal. 3:21). We cannot have a relationship with the Law (a set of standards). Trying to hit the mark apart from a living relationship with God leads to anger, fear, and frustration (Rom. 4:15; 7:24).

The ultimate attempt to measure-up or be good enough manifests itself as religious effort or self-effort (Col. 2:20-23). In this fleshly way of living, we try to be acceptable to God by following the moral law. By God's design, His Laws were never meant to make us acceptable (John 5:39-40).

A mask covers up what is underneath. Masks become very useful when operating in a system that focuses on outward appearance and performance. If we do not believe we measure up on the inside, we can still wear masks so, hopefully, no one will be able to see our faults and reject us.

WHAT DOES LIVING BY A LAW SYSTEM PRODUCE?

Trying to live by any law system can produce unhealthy pride, or self-righteousness. The focus shifts to what I can do instead of what Christ has already done (Gal. 2:21). Those who are more successful in keeping laws will struggle with pride to a greater degree (Luke 18:9-14; Phil. 3:6).

No one can keep God's Laws perfectly (Rom. 3:19-20, 23). When we inevitably fall short of the standards, principles, or expectations of laws, those same laws declare us failures (Gal. 3:10). This failure brings shame, guilt, and condemnation (Rom. 4:15; 5:13).

Operating under law also encourages us to wear masks. Under this system, our worth is determined by our performance. The better we perform, the more value we believe we possess (Matt. 6:1; John 12:43). This belief is a deception (Gal. 6:3). Because we cannot succeed in this system, we cling to a false sense of worth by hiding our failures behind achievements. We fear others will reject us if they see our failures.

Through the flesh, our expectations become a law system of our own design, and as a result, we place others and/or ourselves in a system of performance. If our expectations are met, we feel worthwhile and accepted (blessed); if our expectations go unmet, we feel worth-less and rejected (cursed). This system is not empowered by love. Session 19 will cover in detail the effect of a law system on our relationships.

WHAT RESOURCES ARE EMPLOYED WHEN WE LIVE BY A LAW SYSTEM?

The main resource for living by a law system is the flesh. The desires of the flesh go against our godly desires (Gal. 5:16-17). Flesh, whether it looks good (religious flesh) or looks bad (immoral flesh), remains flesh. It lacks the power to enable us to continually do what is right (Rom. 8:3). The flesh will never supply true life (John 6:63).

When we walk after the flesh, we look to our physical self for strength. The old, false adage that "God helps those who help themselves" suggests we should try hard and then God will help us where we are not strong enough. This adage may sound good, but it completely contradicts biblical truth. The way we have learned to help ourselves is not always God's way (Prov. 14:12). A law system keeps us focused on self-effort to attain a fulfilled life.

> Depending on the flesh is looking to this material world to try to get our needs met. For more information on the flesh, see Session 7.

TIME FOR A NEW SYSTEM

As covered in Session 5, God designed humanity for a receiving system and not an achieving system. Adam chose achievement. Later, God established a covenant based on a law system with the nation of Israel. That covenant was designed to be replaced because Israel could not achieve righteousness by keeping the Law (Jer. 31:31-34; Heb. 8:13). God became a man (Jesus) to fulfill the Law (Matt. 5:17; Heb. 2:17). With His death, He met the final requirement of the Law and established the new covenant of grace which is offered to everyone (Heb. 7:18-22, 26-28; 10:1-10).

WHAT IS A GRACE SYSTEM?

The grace system is an unconditional, receiving system based on God's unmerited favor. Blessings under the Old Covenant Law were based on individual performance, whereas, blessings under the New Covenant of grace are gifted as a result of Christ's performance (Rom. 4:13-16; 8:3-4). At the moment of salvation, God blesses the believer with every spiritual blessing (Eph. 1:3).

Grace is personified in Jesus Christ (John 1:17). He said that He came to give life (John 10:10), not to judge the world (John 3:17). Jesus also said when we look at Him, we see the Father (John 14:7-10). God's grace, as seen in Jesus Christ, reveals His heart toward us. He wants us to know Him, and thereby experience life (John 17:3).

> "For the Law was given through Moses; grace and truth were realized through Jesus Christ." - John 1:17

HOW DID GOD TRANSFER US FROM A LAW SYSTEM TO A GRACE SYSTEM?

In Adam, we were married to the law system. Therefore, the only way to be separated from our bride (the law) was by death. Since the law cannot die, we had to die. Now we are married to another – Christ (Rom. 7:1-6). God has taken us out of Adam (death) and placed us into Christ (life) (Rom. 5:12-21; 1 Cor. 15:22; Col. 1:13). This transfer is the work of God's grace through Christ.

"Therefore, my brethren, you also were made to die to the Law through the body of Christ, that you might be joined to another, to Him who was raised from the dead, that we might bear fruit for God." - Romans 7:4

Through the death of Christ, our old nature (in Adam) was crucified with Christ (Session 8). Through the resurrection of Christ, we were raised as a new creature (Session 9). This new creature is no longer under law but under grace (Rom. 6:14; 10:4). Through the ascension of Christ, we are seated with Him in the heavenly places (Eph. 2:6).

ILLUSTRATION: MARRIED TO MR. LAW OR MR. GRACE (ROM. 7:1-6)?

"for it is God who is at work in you, both to will and to work for His good pleasure." - Philippians 2:13

WHAT DOES IT MEAN TO LIVE BY GRACE?

Grace provides everything the Law could not. The grace of God gives us the desire to do what is right (Rom. 6:17-18; Titus 2:11-14). Christ's life in us is the grace we need to live the Christian life (2 Cor. 9:8). After receiving our new spirit and nature by faith, the indwelling life of Jesus (Holy Spirit) puts His desires in our hearts which lead us inwardly to deny ungodliness (Ezek. 36:27; Rom. 5:5; 8:2).

Not only does grace grant us new desires which line up with God's perfect Law, but grace is also the power of Christ working in us to live His life (2 Cor. 12:9; 2 Tim. 1:7). It is impossible to live the Christian life apart from Christ (John 15:5; 2 Cor. 3:5). God's grace gives us that strength (Heb. 13:9). Through the abundance of the gift of grace (Rom. 5:17), we can manifest Christ's life in our earthly vessels (2 Cor. 4:7).

Grace sets us free from condemnation, slavery to sin, and bondage to law (Acts 13:39; Rom. 6:7; 8:1; Gal. 5:1). True freedom is loving others unconditionally (John 13:34-35; 15:12-13; Rom. 15:7; 1 John 3:16, 23) without the legalistic constraints of performance that leads to judging and condemning (Gal. 6:1-5; Phil. 2:3-4). Freedom allows us to operate out of our true desires, expressed as the fruit of the Spirit. This expression of our desires is not governed by law (Gal. 5:18, 22-23).

> "For if by the transgression of the one, death reigned through the one, much more those who receive the abundance of grace and of the gift of righteousness will reign in life through the One, Jesus Christ."
> - Romans 5:17

ILLUSTRATION: TWO SYSTEMS OF LIVING

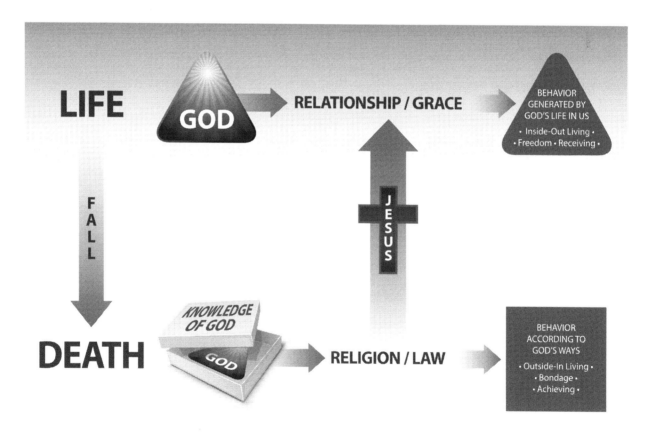

SUMMARY

Our relationship with God is no longer achieved by performance in a law system. We who are in Christ now enjoy a relationship characterized by God's grace. This New Covenant is determined by who He is and what He has already accomplished (performed for us) and then gifted to us in Christ.

TRANSFORM

1. What laws have I tried to keep?

_____

_____

_____

_____

_____

_____

_____

_____

2. What masks do I use to hide my failure to perform?

_____

_____

_____

_____

_____

_____

_____

_____

3. What beliefs lead me to operate under a law system even though I have been set free?

_____

_____

_____

_____

_____

_____

_____

4. In what ways can I transition from a law system to a grace system?

_____

_____

_____

_____

_____

5. Take some time to listen. What is the Holy Spirit telling me in this session?

_____

_____

_____

_____

_____

6. How will the Holy Spirit's revelation impact my beliefs, choices, and behaviors?

_____

_____

_____

_____

_____

 **PRAY**

Father, thank You for rescuing me from the kingdom of darkness and transferring me to the kingdom of Your Beloved Son. Thank You for giving me an abundance of grace and the gift of righteousness so that I can reign in life through Jesus Christ. Thank You that I am no longer under a law system but can enjoy the freedom of Your grace. Your life gives me everything law could not. Amen.

RELATING UNCONDITIONALLY
Sharing Life

CONNECT

- What has God revealed to you since we last met?

- What conditions or expectations do people place on others?

- How are relationships affected by conditions or expectations?

- What does a grace filled relationship look like?

RENEW

TWO SYSTEMS

The last session explained the difference between law and grace. We examined how we were freed from a law system and entered into a new covenant relationship with God based on His unconditional love and acceptance through grace. Grace is the much better covenant. It is based on what God has done and focuses on identity – who we are in Christ (Session 10).

Because God placed us into a new covenant with Him based on grace, His desire is that we also relate to others based on unconditional love and acceptance (Rom. 12:10; 15:7; Eph. 4:2, 32). We express love spontaneously when we submit our will to the Holy Spirit. However, we can still be tempted to walk after the flesh and choose to conduct our relationships with others by imposing laws (Gal. 5:16-18).

WHAT DO RELATIONSHIPS LOOK LIKE UNDER LAW?

EXPECTATIONS...

An expectation is a strong belief that something should happen or be a certain way. Relationships under law are driven by expectations. Those expectations, whether spoken or unspoken (imagined), become the standards which determine the success of the relationship. If the other person is fulfilling our expectations, then we are happy; if they are not, then we are unhappy. The fleshly goal of getting others to meet our needs drives us to place expectations on them.

When an expectation becomes a law in the relationship, that expectation must be met. If the expectation is not met, a law has been broken, and consequences occur. No amount of excuses, reasons, or explanations can rationalize the infraction. This system focuses the relationship on living up to other's expectations. Unmet expectations bring disappointment which results in rejection, whether direct or indirect (Prov. 13:12).

PERFORMANCE...

The law system is based on performance. In Session 18 we learned the purpose of God's Law. Just as the Law never made it possible for the Israelites to have a consistent, intimate relationship with God, so too instituting behavioral standards (law or expectations) on others prevents intimacy between people.

A law system of expectations forces others to try to be good enough to gain our love and acceptance. "How much is enough?" then becomes the pressing question. Law demands perfect performance for acceptance. People operating under law-based relationships end up concentrating on the short-comings of others instead of their virtues.

SYSTEM OF FAILURE...

Relationships based on a law system will fail. Law points out flaws but does nothing to empower the other person. The focus is not on their identity, but strictly on their behavior. Under a law system, no one measures up all the time.

Law brings about anger, wrath, sadness, hurt, and frustration in relationships (Rom. 5:20a). The person who places an expectation on another becomes angry or hurt when the expectation goes unmet (Rom. 4:15a; 1 Cor. 15:56b). This unmet expectation leads to frustration, wrath, and retribution (James 4:1-2).

Living underneath another's expectations sets us on an emotional roller coaster. If we perform to their standards, then we feel good about ourselves. If we miss the mark others set for us, then our sense of worth is diminished.

Putting others under expectations for acceptance or trying to live up to other's expectations is idolatry, which always brings death and destruction to relationships. God designed us to look to Him alone for worth and value (1 Tim. 6:17). He created us to relate to Him by grace through faith alone and, in turn, relate to all others with unconditional love and grace (John 13:34; 1 John 4:19).

People who relate to others on the basis of expectations and laws often communicate with a critical tongue. Belittling, condemning, demanding, fault-finding, nagging, and sarcasm discourage others and destroy intimacy and harmony.

"And the tongue is a fire, the very world of iniquity; the tongue is set among our members as that which defiles the entire body, and sets on fire the course of our life, and is set on fire by hell." - James 3:6

WHAT DO RELATIONSHIPS LOOK LIKE UNDER GRACE?

EXPECTATIONS...

Paul said we have been given the abundance of grace to reign in life through Jesus Christ (Rom. 5:17). We can relate to others through the grace of God instead of focusing on their performance. Through Christ, we can value others apart from their behavior. We view them through love instead of judging them by their actions (Rom. 15:7; 1 Cor. 4:1-5; 13:5; 2 Cor. 5:14-16a).

A key component of grace is summed up in the word "unconditional," which means there is no condition that determines who WE are and how WE love. A person who operates relationally in grace gives love and acceptance out of who they are and not as a response to another's behavior (1 Pet. 3:8-9).

PERFORMANCE....

Grace is personified in the person of Jesus Christ (John 1:17). We can look at His earthly life and observe how He related to those around Him. Our ability to relate to others like Jesus is only possible through the enabling power of the Holy Spirit (2 Cor. 9:8; Eph. 3:20; 1 John 4:7). Jesus told His disciples He must go away so that the Helper would come (John 16:7). We now have Christ living His life in us (Session 9), which means we now have grace personified living through us (Gal. 2:20; Eph. 3:16-19). His perfect performance on our behalf, as seen in His life, death, and resurrection, is now manifested in our lives when we submit to Him (1 Cor. 15:10; 2 Cor. 4:6-12; Col. 1:29; James 4:7).

Paul stated in Galatians 5:22-23, "But the fruit of the Spirit is love, joy, peace, patience, kindness, goodness, faithfulness, gentleness, self-control..." This fruit is reflected in our behavior as we relate to others under grace (Session 12). In Ephesians 4:2 Paul adds humility and tolerance to the list. Under grace, tolerance looks like love. Under law, it looks like "putting up with others" while having an attitude of intolerance. Tolerance allows God to fully reveal His character in us and others without judging or condemning.

SYSTEM OF SUCCESS...

When all our needs are met in Christ, we are free to give love unconditionally to others. Regardless of how others treat us, we can always respond the way we want to be treated (Luke 6:31; 1 Thess. 5:15; 1 Pet. 3:8-9). A person filled with the grace of God is quick to forgive (Acts 7:60) and quick to ask forgiveness. Grace enables very healthy and intimate relationships (Matt. 5:44).

Paul gave a beautiful picture of graceful relationships in Philippians 2:1-4. We can share the same love and mind because we have God's love (Rom. 5:5; 1 John 4:16-19) and the mind of Christ (1 Cor. 2:16). Even though we have different personalities and sometimes share different opinions, we can be united in spirit (Acts 1:14; Rom. 15:5; Eph. 2:18). Our love for one another enables us to see our unity in Christ (Eph. 4:3). In graceful relationships, people put others before themselves (1 Cor. 10:24).

Unconditional love and service encourages others and provides a safe place to grow in grace and overcome their struggles (1 Cor. 13:5; I John 4:18). This safe place is characterized by gentleness and freedom from guilt and condemnation (Rom. 6:14; 8:1; Gal. 6:1).

"To sum up, all of you be harmonious, sympathetic, brotherly, kindhearted, and humble in spirit; not returning evil for evil or insult for insult, but giving a blessing instead; for you were called for the very purpose that you might inherit a blessing." - 1 Peter 3:8-9

Graceful

One way we give grace to others in relationships is through our speech.

"Let no unwholesome word proceed from your mouth, but only such a word as is good for edification according to the need of the moment, that it may give grace to those who hear." - Ephesians 4:29

"But encourage one another day after day, as long as it is still called 'Today,' lest any one of you be hardened by the deceitfulness of sin."

- Hebrews 3:13

HOW DOES ACCOUNTABILITY FIT INTO RELATING UNCONDITIONALLY?

Ultimately, everyone is accountable to God (Ps. 94:2; Rom. 14:12-13; 1 Pet. 4:5). He is the One who is in control (Prov. 19:21; Eph. 4:6), and He knows and understands the thoughts, emotions, and intentions of our hearts (1 Chr. 28:9). His amazing attributes qualify Him as the one and only lawgiver and judge (Is. 33:22; Jer. 17:10; Heb. 4:13; James 4:12).

In healthy relationships, mutual accountability is natural. Instead of making and enforcing laws on others, accountability among believers involves encouraging, exhorting, praying for, and restoring each other in love (Gal. 6:1; 2 Tim. 4:2; Heb. 3:13; 10:24-25; James 5:16). Just as we encourage others to set their minds on things above, we want to practice the same (Session 14).

Healthy accountability encourages (1 Thess. 5:11, 14) by reminding others of their true identity in Christ and placing the focus on Christ in them (Col. 1:27). The apostle Paul held the Corinthians accountable in this way when they continued to sin (1 Cor. 3). Accountability does not mean there will not be slips or failures, but it does mean we will assume the best of the other person regardless of unmet expectations (Prov. 27:17; 1 Cor. 9:12; Gal. 6:1-2; Col. 3:16).

Accountability becomes an exercise in futility when it focuses on behavior and uses fear, shame, and guilt as motivation to stop sinning. The shame and guilt felt by the person who must report their sins leads to the temptation to develop flesh patterns such as lying, avoidance, mask wearing, etc. Instead of decreasing these sin patterns, new ones are added. Graceful accountability addresses behavior by reminding the one struggling of their identity in Christ (1 Cor. 3:16; 6:16-20).

SUMMARY

Relationships based on expectations (laws) are unhealthy and produce anger, hurt, frustration, and sorrow. Relationships based on grace release others from the performance expectations of living under law. Giving grace to others fosters healthy relationships by providing an atmosphere where intimacy can flourish and people can grow in Christ.

TRANSFORM

WHAT ARE MY EXPECTATIONS FOR OTHERS? HOW HAVE I MADE THOSE EXPECTATIONS A LAW?

Use the forms on the following two pages to think through any expectations you may be placing on others. First, think about an important person in your life and place their name in the box at the top of the chart. Then along the bottom, enter categories of behavior that you expect from them (see example on the following page). Next, rate them on their level of success in each area, based on your opinion (scale of 1 to 10). You can either consider overall performance or a moment when you were most frustrated with them. Draw a horizontal line at the number you chose. Shade in the space below the line. When finished, use the questions on the following pages to analyze the results.

DISCOVERING EXPECTATIONS WORKSHEET

Use the blank charts to analyze any expectations you may have for yourself or significant people in your life. More forms are on the back of this page.

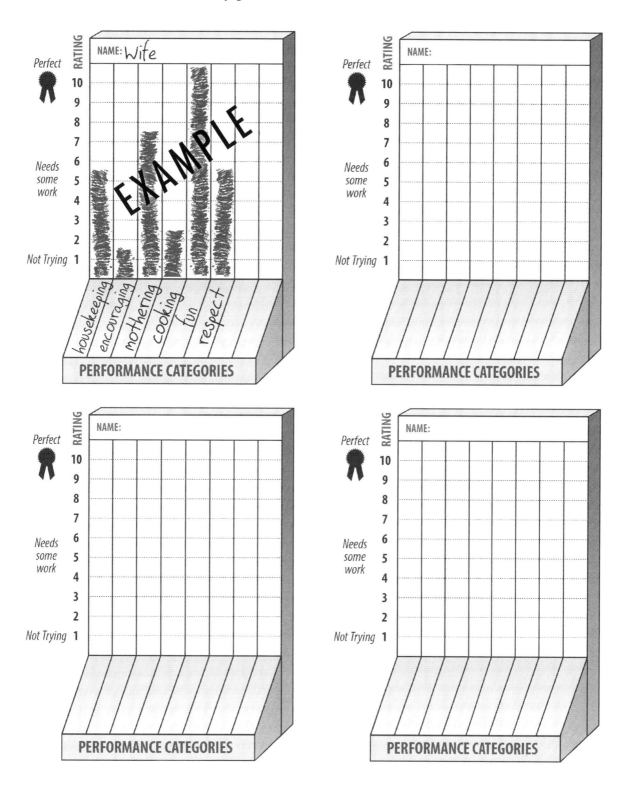

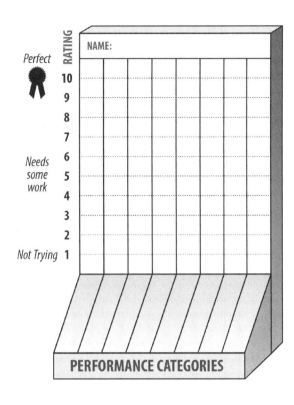

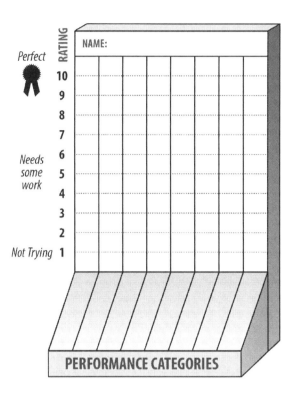

1. What do the various ratings say about my expectations, disappointments, and rejection (directly or indirectly) of this person?

_____

_____

_____

_____

_____

_____

2. In what ways do I try to get my needs met through my most intimate relationships?

_____

_____

_____

_____

_____

_____

3. What is standing in the way of surrendering my expectations of others to God?

_____

_____

_____

_____

_____

_____

_____

_____

4. In what ways have I expressed grace in my relationships?

_____

_____

_____

_____

_____

_____

_____

_____

 **PRAY**

Father, thank You that I am righteous in Jesus Christ. You love and accept me completely with no other requirement or addition needed. I freely receive Your love. I surrender my will to Yours, allowing Your will and purposes to be accomplished in and through me. I depend on You for my life and to meet all my needs. I respond in obedience to Your voice and will. Show me where I have imposed a law-based system on those around me. (Name specific people if led to do so.) Lead me to see these people through Your eyes and live with them through Your grace. Thank You for extending so much grace to me. Amen.

EQUIPPING OTHERS
Multiplying Life

CONNECT

- What has God revealed to you since we last met?

- Who has influenced you in a way that spurred growth in your Christian walk?

- In what ways have they influenced you?

RENEW

GOD'S GOAL FOR HUMANITY

God originally designed creation to be an expression of Himself. Habakkuk 2:14 gives us insight into His goal for the world when God says, "For the earth will be filled with the knowledge of the glory of the LORD, as the waters cover the sea." Psalm 72:19 also conveys this goal when it proclaims, "And blessed be His glorious name forever; And may the whole earth be filled with His glory. Amen and Amen." God's heart is for all of humanity to be containers and expressers of His life, thus glorifying Him (Session 4). Even though all humanity chose to rebel against His purposes, God's goal remains the same (Is. 43:13).

In Revelation 13:8, we see that God's plan for accomplishing His goal always centered on Jesus Christ. At the right time in history (Gal. 4:4), God's light of life entered a dark world in the person of Jesus (John 1:4, 9). He paid the price for the sin of humanity and invited everyone back into His life through relationship with the Father, Son, and Holy Spirit (Sessions 8 and 9). But Jesus was just one man. How could He accomplish God's goal of filling all the earth with the glory of God? What was, and continues to be, His plan?

"to the only God our Savior, through Jesus Christ our Lord, be glory, majesty, dominion and authority, before all time and now and forever. Amen." - Jude 1:25

"but you will receive power when the Holy Spirit has come upon you; and you shall be My witnesses both in Jerusalem, and in all Judea and Samaria, and even to the remotest part of the earth." - Acts 1:8

After Jesus ascended to Heaven, He chose to place Himself inside His disciples in the form of the Holy Spirit and partner with them in multiplying His life and love around the world (Luke 24:48-49; John 14:16-20; 1 John 5:12). When the life of Christ entered those first disciples, they instantly became a light for others, which was exactly what Jesus told them would happen before He left (Acts 1:8). As they chose to live from the inside out, submitting their will to the Holy Spirit, others saw the fruit of their lives and heard their testimony about Jesus (Acts 4:13). Many who saw and heard placed their faith and trust in Jesus, received the Holy Spirit, and became full of Christ's light and love (Matt. 5:16; Eph. 5:8-10). When these new disciples experienced life in Christ, they in turn began equipping other believers (Acts 2:42; 6:4). The life of God began to multiply and grow (Acts 6:7).

That same plan for spreading God's life and love throughout the earth continues today (Matt. 28:19). When we gave our life to Christ, we entered His family. We became sons and daughters of light by receiving the life of Christ (Session 10). Now, the Holy Spirit invites and leads us to partner with Him in multiplying His life so that the whole world is filled with the glory of God (1 Cor. 15:28; Phil. 2:9-11). When we are living from the inside out, we want to join in God's plan and express the good news of Christ's life which we received from God (2 Cor. 4:7; 5:14-15; Titus 2:14; 1 Pet. 2:9).

ILLUSTRATION: MULTIPLICATION

Through our display of Christ's life, others will see and choose to believe and receive eternal life. We can then equip them for life in Christ by giving them the truth in love. As they step into their new identity in Christ, they will also share the life they have received. This continues the process of multiplication that first began with Jesus Christ.

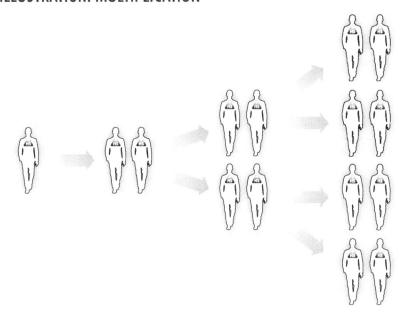

LIFE SHARED AND MULTIPLIED IN RELATIONSHIPS

Because God exists in relationship (the Trinity), He designed us to intentionally share life with others in relationship (John 13:34-35). Every interaction in a relationship provides an opportunity to express the life and love of God (1 John 4:7). As we journey through life, we meet and interact with unbelievers and believers. With unbelievers, we have the opportunity to show them God's love and give witness to the reason for our hope, faith, peace, and love (Rom. 1:5; 1 Pet. 3:15). As we share life, we invite them to accept God's free gift of life through Jesus (evangelism) (2 Cor. 5:20).

The Holy Spirit also directs us into intentional relationships with others who have placed their faith and trust in Jesus. All believers are at various stages in their spiritual growth (Session 13). When we encounter mature believers, we have the privilege to encourage them by spurring them on in love to continue walking in the truth, living out of their identity in Christ, and submitting their will to the Holy Spirit (1 Thess. 5:11; Heb. 3:13; 10:24-25). In addition, connecting with new or immature believers gives us the chance to equip them by helping them grow in their knowledge and understanding of the finished work of Christ in them (discipleship) (Rom. 14:1; 15:1-2; Col. 3:16).

"and let us consider how to stimulate one another to love and good deeds, not forsaking our own assembling together, as is the habit of some, but encouraging one another; and all the more as you see the day drawing near."
- Hebrews 10:24-25

ILLUSTRATION: SHARING AND EQUIPPING IN RELATIONSHIPS

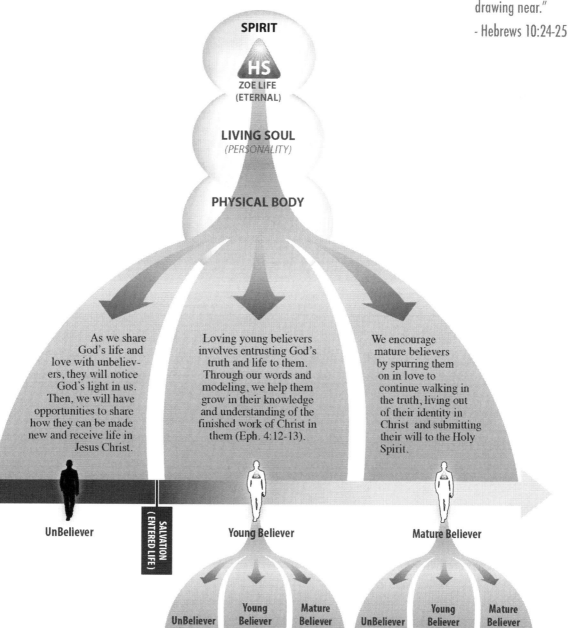

"And Jesus said to them, 'Follow Me, and I will make you become fishers of men.'" - Mark 1:17

OUR EXAMPLE FOR LIFE EQUIPPING – JESUS

Jesus was the first discipler or "Life Equipper." While He walked this earth, He showed us how to multiply His life by first walking in intimacy with the Father and then intentionally engaging others (those who the Father sent to Him) in healthy relationships (John 13:13-15; 17:6-8). As He spent time with his disciples, Jesus equipped them for life by communicating truth wrapped in love and grace (Luke 4:22; John 8:1-11; Eph. 4:15). Now that He lives in us, we also naturally desire to equip others in the same way, as we submit our will to Him and live from the inside out (Matt. 28:19-20; Luke 6:40; John 20:21; 1 Cor. 11:1).

WALKING IN INTIMACY WITH THE FATHER

"With all prayer and petition pray at all times in the Spirit, and with this in view, be on the alert with all perseverance and petition for all the saints," - Ephesians 6:18

Life equipping begins with an intimate walk with God (Sessions 4, 11, and 13). The Bible directs us to live in constant communion with the Father just as Jesus did (Eph. 6:18; 1 Thess. 5:17). He only acted as the Father directed Him (John 5:19). He only spoke as the Father prompted Him (John 4:34; 12:49; 14:10). Jesus walked in perfect intimacy and communication with the Father (John 17:21). As Jesus went about His daily ministry, the Father brought hurting people to Him and, at the same time, gave Him the words of truth to share with them. Through intimate fellowship with our Heavenly Father, we will know how He wants us to use our mouth, hands, and feet to display and multiply His life and love in the world (Luke 21:14-15; Col. 1:9-10).

INTENTIONALLY ENGAGING OTHERS IN HEALTHY RELATIONSHIPS

"So then, those who had received his word were baptized; and that day there were added about three thousand souls. They were continually devoting themselves to the apostles' teaching and to fellowship, to the breaking of bread and to prayer. Everyone kept feeling a sense of awe; and many wonders and signs were taking place through the apostles." - Acts 2:41-43

Life equipping is most effective within healthy, intentional relationships rooted in love and grace (Session 19). Spending time together eating, talking, working, praying, playing, and serving provides the framework for building healthy relationships and communicating transformational truth.

When Jesus began equipping his disciples, He did not start a college or seminary where His followers could show up for class to listen to His teachings. Instead, He picked a few men to live life with Him and communicated truth experientially as they went from town to town (Mark 3:14). Occasionally, Jesus sat with groups of people and taught them, but He spent much of his time just living life with His disciples and building relationships (Mark 6:30-32).

GROWING TOGETHER IN LOVE AND TRUTH

Building on the foundation of walking in intimacy with God and intentionally engaging others in healthy relationships, the Holy Spirit will move us to share truth with others. Paul told Timothy in 2 Timothy 2:1-2, "You therefore, my son, be strong in the grace that is in Christ Jesus. The things which you have heard from me in the presence of many witnesses, entrust these to faithful men who will be able to teach others also."

Communicating truth is very effective when packaged within the spiritual fruit of love. Truth spoken without love can be annoying, harsh, abrasive, and damaging (1 Cor. 13:1-3; 16:14). As Jesus built relationships, He listened attentively and used questions masterfully to get to the heart of the person (Matt. 9:3-5; 16:13-17; Mark 11:29-30). He communicated truth in ways that were relevant to the person in their journey, showing them support and encouragement (Matt. 28:20b; John 16:33). Jesus served others instead of demanding to be served (Matt. 20:28). His heart was always to build up and establish others, not tear them down. As Jesus expressed His perfect love, people were drawn to Him and listened to what He said (Matt. 7:28-29; John 1:14; 6:67-68).

SUMMARY

God desires the whole earth to be filled with His glory (His life). Through Jesus Christ, God has placed His life inside of us. A burning desire grows for others to experience Christ's life as we come to know and believe the truth about God, our design and purpose, and our relationship with God in Christ. God's glory spreads as we share Christ's life with others and equip them (make disciples). This process results in the multiplication and maturing of the body of Christ. Life Equippers enjoy an intimate walk with God, intentionally engage others in healthy relationships, and grow together in love and truth. Through the model Jesus displayed, we can share life with unbelievers and equip believers as they grow in their knowledge and understanding of Christ as their life.

> "... speaking the truth in love, we are to grow up in all aspects into Him who is the head, even Christ, from whom the whole body, being fitted and held together by what every joint supplies, according to the proper working of each individual part, causes the growth of the body for the building up of itself in love."
> - Ephesians 4:14-16

TRANSFORM

1. What hindrances might keep me from equipping others?

_____

_____

_____

_____

_____

2. What current relationships do I have where I can express His life and love and share what God has done in my life?

_____

_____

_____

_____

_____

3. Take some time to listen to the Spirit. Is He placing a new person on my heart with whom I could build a healthy relationship? If so, who?

_____

_____

_____

_____

_____

4. In what ways could I go about building that relationship?

_____

_____

_____

_____

_____

 **PRAYER**

Father, I enjoy You in this moment. Right now. Right here. I love You for You and not for anything You might do for me. You have already done all for me, and I thank You. I receive Your love and love You back with that same love. I surrender to You. I depend on You to meet my needs and to be the source of my life. Remind me of Your truths and my true identity as a child of God. I set my mind on You and embrace Your truths. Now guide me in this journey regarding what You would have me do next. Open my eyes to where You are currently working. Lead me into conversations and to relationships where I can express Your life and love. I commit my ways to You and trust You to give me the desires of my heart and direction to my paths. Amen

GRAND SUMMARY

GOD'S ORIGINAL DESIGN (HOW GOD MADE US)

God is life, spirit, and love. He is also the creator and the personal relator. All He creates flows from His essence. Knowing and possessing God's character and nature is essential to experiencing a personal relationship and intimate fellowship with Him.[1]

Adam and Eve were made in the image of God, thus their core identity was "child of God." God uniquely designed humans as living beings who are each a spirit and soul (in His image), dwelling in a physical body and expressing themselves through their soul (with thoughts, emotions, and choices) and body (according to His likeness). As a result of this design, Adam and Eve enjoyed a personal relationship and intimate fellowship with God.[2] God designed humanity with needs only He can meet. This design established an intimate relationship characterized and enhanced by man's dependence on God's provision. Adam and Eve lived in a healthy relationship with God (loving Him), with themselves (loving themselves), and with each other (based on unconditional love and enjoyment of His overflow to each other).[3]

God created man and woman to enjoy intimate fellowship with Him and to display His life (glorify God). Paul describes the mechanics of glorifying God as the principle of the mind: 1) we receive a thought from the Spirit, 2) we process that thought, 3) we choose to submit our will to His direction, and 4) we carry out that action empowered by the Spirit. This process describes how to love God and, in turn, love ourselves and others. When we rest in God's provision and move only under His direction, we live from the inside out, accomplishing God's purpose for humanity.[4]

HUMANITY'S FALL (WHAT WENT WRONG)

The two trees in the middle of the Garden of Eden represent a choice between two systems for living. The tree of life represents an option to trust God which leads to meaning, purpose, and fulfillment. The tree of the knowledge of good and evil represents an option to rely on perception, experience, and self-reasoning apart from God, resulting in death.[5]

Adam and Eve chose to eat from the tree of the knowledge of good and evil. As a consequence of the Fall, they lost God's life, resulting in spiritual death and separation from God. Their physical bodies began to decay. They began to look for sources other than God to meet their needs. Their spiritual death produced a sin nature that changed their identity from children of God to children of Satan. The law of sin entered their bodies, and they developed coping mechanisms to try to meet their needs in the flesh. Adam's and Eve's fallen (condemned) condition has been passed down to all humanity.[6]

Born with a nature that is hostile toward God's love, acceptance, and value, everyone develops ways (flesh patterns) to make life work and meet their own needs apart from God. Whether confidence based or shame based, all flesh patterns result from false beliefs which lead to self-effort and futility.[7]

LIFE RESTORED (HOW GOD MADE US RIGHT)

God, in the person of Jesus, has resolved the two problems that kept us from an intimate relationship with Him. He dealt with our sins (problem #1) when He became flesh and blood, fulfilling the Law, and paid the penalty for sin through the sacrifice of Himself. He removed our fallen and natural identity in Adam (problem #2) by crucifying our old self in Christ. Our response is to believe and receive God's provision for our salvation.[8]

At the moment of salvation, we were made new creations indwelt by the Holy Spirit, and we entered into a new covenant with God characterized by abundant life. The old, sinful nature (old self) was exchanged for a new nature so we can naturally and uniquely express Christ's life in every action. We were given a full, spiritual inheritance with the guarantee that all needs will be met in Christ.[9] At salvation, we exchanged fathers - from Satan to God. Changing fathers produced a family exchange – from Adam's family to God's family. Our identity is now a dearly loved child of God who is righteous and fully accepted. As God's children we have an identity that is defined by who He is, by what He has done, and by His opinion of us.[10]

God desires a close relationship with His children because He is love. Our lives together with God are characterized by His leadership and our dependence. He leads us through love into greater intimacy with Him and empowers us (through the Holy Spirit), to follow Him. God fosters intimacy with us by speaking to us with His loving voice through the Holy Spirit. As we spend time with God in prayer and in the Scriptures, we learn to distinguish His voice from the voices of Satan and his demons. The Holy Spirit speaks to us directly in our minds by giving us thoughts, images, or impressions. He also communicates through the Scriptures, other people, and other means. Each of us is on a unique personal journey of life with God.[11]

LIFE EXPRESSED (HOW WE EXPERIENCE LIFE EVERYDAY)

God designed us to uniquely express Christ's life. The Bible calls this expression "bearing fruit." Christ's life in each of us is our life. It flows from us naturally and spontaneously as we submit our will to His. Every believer is endowed with unique talents, abilities, and spiritual gifts. These enable the believer to individually express Christ's life for the benefit and edification of Christ's body - the church. Our expression of Christ's life is most evident when we focus on the truth and enjoy intimacy with the Father.[12]

While our spiritual growth is caused by God, we can foster this growth through spiritual disciplines which include Bible study, worship, prayer, fasting, giving thanks, etc. These activities provide opportunities to deepen our intimacy with God. We do not engage in them in order to earn God's acceptance or to achieve righteousness through self-effort. Spiritual disciplines, when carried out under the direction of the Holy Spirit, become ways of enjoying His presence and a means of knowing Him more intimately.[13]

Christ secured the victory once and for all at the cross, but He has not yet banished Satan and the forces of evil in this world. God made us new spiritually, but He left us temporarily in our dying bodies with a choice to live either from the inside out or from the outside in. God has not erased our memories, instead He asks and instructs us to consider ourselves dead to the old fleshly ways and alive to His life within us. The war is being waged each and every day in our minds. When we reject the lies, believe the truth, and move under the direction and power of the Holy Spirit, we walk in the victory that is ours in Christ.[14] Understanding our flesh is crucial to recognizing the lies from the enemy. We can take those lies captive and believe the truth revealed by the Holy Spirit.[15]

Because we still live in a fallen world and sometimes choose to walk after the flesh, we will face difficulties. God uses burdens in our lives to bring about brokenness. In the midst of suffering He often reveals counterfeit need-meeters and our futile strategies of dependence on our own resources. God leads us to surrender our rights, allowing us to experience His abundant supply. As we surrender rights, we experience the love, joy, and peace found in Christ's life.[16]

If we walk after the flesh, we will hurt and offend each other. God's full forgiveness and our new nature in Christ enable us to forgive. We can choose to forgive the offender by releasing the debt owed and letting go of the hurt and anger. When we offend another, we can seek forgiveness by taking responsibility for our action and asking for forgiveness. We can choose to surrender to the Holy Spirit and express Christ's life through forgiveness, whether a relationship is reconciled or not.[17]

Our relationship with God is no longer achieved by performance in a law system. We who are in Christ now enjoy a relationship characterized by God's grace. This New Covenant is determined by who He is and what He has already accomplished (performed for us) and then gifted to us in Christ.[18]

Now that God relates to us through grace, the Holy Spirit leads us to relate to others in the same way. Relationships based on expectations (laws) are unhealthy and produce anger, hurt, frustration, and sorrow. Relationships based on grace releases others from the performance expectations of living under law. Giving grace to others fosters healthy relationships by providing an atmosphere where intimacy can flourish and people can grow in Christ.[19]

A burning desire grows for others to experience Christ's life as we come to know and believe the truth about God, our design and purpose, and our relationship with God in Christ. To this end, the Spirit empowers us to be life equippers who make disciples through multiplying and maturing the body of Christ.[20]

* The notation numbers are the session numbers from which the summary was taken.

GUIDE TO ILLUSTRATIONS

PURPOSE OF THIS GUIDE

This Guide to Illustrations is a tool for you to better understand and explain the illustrations (diagrams) throughout the *Living in Jesus Participant's Guide*.

HOW TO USE THIS GUIDE

The illustrations are designed to enhance comprehension of the written content. This guide will help you link the session content with the illustrations.

The layout of this guide gives you a concise and user-friendly explanation of each part in the illustrations. The text boxes are numbered to provide a recommended sequence to progress through each illustration.

Several of the illustrations build on one another as you progress through *Living in Jesus*. Where parts have been discussed before, explanations are not repeated. When applicable, a connection to the previous illustrations is found beneath the title.

The explanations are not intended to be exhaustive; therefore, Scripture references are not usually included. Supporting Scriptures are found in the Renew section of the sessions.

LIST OF ILLUSTRATIONS

The page numbers listed below correspond to the page numbers where the illustration is used in the *Participant's Guide*.

SESSION 7

SESSION 8

SESSION 9

SESSION 14

SESSION 18

SESSION 20

ILLUSTRATION: HUMANITY'S UNIQUE DESIGN (FROM PG. 9)

(The concept of God [illustrated by the triangle icon] was covered in Session 1. Start with "image" and "likeness" on the right side.)

4

We know that God can hear, see, taste, smell, and touch but with spiritual and not physical senses. God also created humanity with spiritual senses for interacting with Him. Because God is Spirit, He relates to us through our spirit. We can hear His inaudible voice in our minds, see Him through the spiritual eyes of faith, taste and smell His goodness in our spirit and touch and feel Him by faith.

3

God filled and animated Adam and Eve with His breath or Spirit. God empowered them to display His life by placing His Spirit inside them. With His life inside them, they were living in eternal life.

2

God made Adam and Eve in His image as living beings that includes a spirit which is finite and contained (limited to time and space).

5

Our soul is made up of our mind, will, and emotions. With our mind, we think and process thoughts. With our will, we make decisions. With our emotions, we feel. Even though the soul is immaterial (not physical), other people can experience our soul through our interactions in relationships. Another word for soul is personality. Because God created humanity to be expressive creatures, He designed our soul to use our bodies to express our unique spiritual identity. A soul that is connected to God's life is a living soul.

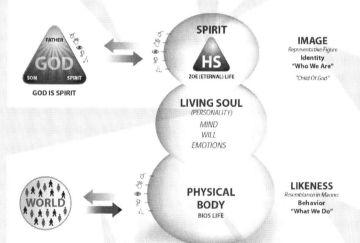

IMAGE
Representative Figure
Identity
"Who We Are"

"Child Of God"

LIKENESS
Resemblance in Manner
Behavior
"What We Do"

6

God created Adam and Eve in His image and according to His likeness. Image has to do with identity. Adam and Eve were created with an identity in their inner being that was a direct reflection of God. Likeness has to do with behavior. Adam and Eve were able to behave like God because they possessed His image. They were identified as children of God, and as such, they behaved like God in their actions. This is called inside-out living.

6

God formed Adam's physical body from the dust of the earth. Our physical bodies are the containers in which we live on this earth.

7

Our body is the instrument we use to interact with the physical world. God gave us five physical senses (sound, sight, taste, smell, and touch) to interact with other people and our physical environment. We have been uniquely designed to manifest God's glory in the physical world and rule over the earth as stewards under God's authority.

ILLUSTRATION: MEN AND WOMEN CREATED WITH NEEDS (FROM PG. 15)

(The concept of God was covered in Session 1.) God creates out of who He is. He exists in relationship (Father, Son, Holy Spirit).

9
What did Adam need from Eve? What did Eve need from Adam? Nothing. Adam and Eve were not capable of meeting each other's needs because God never intended them to be the providers. As containers of God's life, they were filled to overflowing with the Spirit's fruit. This design resulted in them becoming expressers of God's life. Having their needs met by God, Adam and Eve were free to unconditionally gift to each other their desires.

3
God is our provider and is the only One qualified to meet our needs effectively. He created needs that only He could meet in order to display His provision and to cultivate Adam's dependency, trust, surrender, receptivity, and intimacy with God. He met Adam's needs through a personal relationship with intimate fellowship.

6
God also provided all of Eve's needs to create the same relationship He had with Adam, one of dependency, trust, surrender, receptivity, and intimacy. God also met Eve's needs through a personal relationship with intimate fellowship.

1
God created Adam with needs. A need is something we MUST have to live. Our physical needs consist of air, water, food, and rest. Without them we would physically die. Humans also have inner needs.

2
The inner needs of Adam (men) may be listed as: respect, love, acceptance, etc. This list is not all of Adam's needs, but represents a few common ones.

5
God then fashioned Eve. Because God exists in relationship and created man/woman to live in relationship, He made Eve to share life and love with Himself and Adam. He designed Eve to live in intimate relationship with Adam and to work with God in producing more life on earth (procreating).

4
When God met Adam's needs, Adam experienced fulfillment beyond imagination and concluded that he had great value and felt worthwhile.

8
When God met Eve's needs, she experienced fulfillment beyond imagination and concluded that she had great value and felt worthwhile.

7
Eve's (or woman's) needs included love, respect, connectedness, thoughtfulness, kindness, and the needs discussed in the sub-section about her needs.

ILLUSTRATION: THE MECHANICS OF GLORIFYING GOD (FROM PG. 21)

6

Through their God-directed and God-empowered behavior, their purpose of expressing (glorifying/honoring) God on this earth was accomplished.

5

With their behavior, Adam and Eve expected to fulfill their God-given purpose of naturally expressing His life. Their expectations were healthy, loving, and God-initiated.

7

Each time Adam and Eve received of God and gave to God and others, they completed a healthy relationship cycle.

4

Adam and Eve's choice led to a behavior.

1

We have already covered the Concept of God in Session 1, p. 3, and Needs of Humanity in Session 3, p. 15 (the left portion of this illustration).

2

God put thoughts into Adam and Eve's mind about who they were and what to do with their days. They processed those thoughts by checking in with their memories and emotions. Up until the fall, every interaction with God produced a good memory.

3

With their will, Adam and Eve chose to rely upon God and obey His directions.

ILLUSTRATION: HUMANITY AFTER THE FALL (FROM PG. 34)

(This illustration is first introduced and explained in Session 2, pg. 9. The focus here is to illustrate the effects of the fall on humanity.)

2

Adam and Eve separated themselves from God by their choice that resulted in an act of disobedience (sin). God did not change. He pursued them in their fallen state. Adam and Eve changed.

4

Because their spiritual identity changed to reflect Satan's nature, they were now sinners (old self) with a sin nature. When they were alive, godliness and righteousness were natural to their character. After the Fall, the most natural thing for them to do was to sin.

3

Adam and Eve's identity changed. Without God's life (the Holy Spirit), they could not retain their original identity. Having been fathered in nature by Satan, they became children of the devil.

1

After they sinned, life left Adam and Eve. Death is the absence of life. Adam and Eve still had a spirit, but without the Holy Spirit, they were now spiritually dead.

5

Adam and Eve did not lose their souls. However, being cut off from God's life, they changed from living souls to souls that merely existed. Instead of expressing God's life, their souls expressed their sin nature (old self) through their thoughts, emotions, and choices.

9

Before the Fall, Adam and Eve contained God's life, and they were able to interact with Him personally and intimately. Their choices reflected living from the inside-out. After the fall, without God's life inside, they looked to their interaction with the world and the world's system authored by Satan to try to get their needs and desires met. This broken system is called outside-in living.

8

As a result of Adam's sin, the physical world was cursed. This caused the human body to become subject to the contamination of sin and the process of decay and death.

7

The law (principle) of sin entered Adam and Eve's bodies. Paul referred to this indwelling sin as the "law of sin" in Romans 7:23. Indwelling sin can be compared to gravity. Just as gravity pulls our physical bodies downward, indwelling sin pulls us downward to gratify the sinful desires of the flesh.

6

After Adam and Eve lost life, they developed habitual (programmed) coping mechanisms to meet their own needs. The Apostle Paul refers to these coping mechanisms as "the flesh" (to be discussed in more detail in Session 7).

ILLUSTRATION: HUMANITY DIED IN ADAM (FROM PG. 35)

1 God is eternal life (Session 1). Before the Fall, Adam and Eve were designed to live eternally. They were created as creatures to contain God's eternal life.

2 When Adam and Eve disobeyed God, they lost God's life (the Holy Spirit left) which is referred to as "the Fall." They stood condemned and lived in darkness because they were guilty of sinning against God.

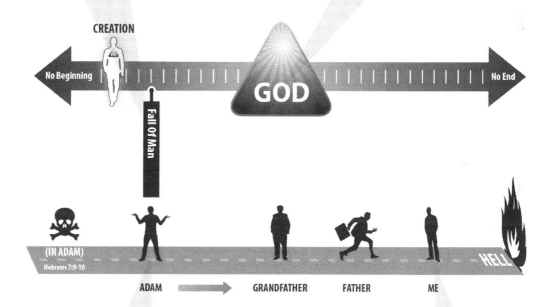

3 When they sinned, Adam and Eve fell from eternal life to eternal death. Hell is the destination of all those who are eternally dead.

4 Because the entire human race descended from Adam, we are all born on the road to hell. When Adam died spiritually, all of humanity died spiritually. When Adam became a sinner, all of humanity became sinners. When Adam's needs went unmet, all of humanity's needs went unmet. When Adam was condemned, all of humanity was condemned.

ILLUSTRATION: A BROKEN SYSTEM OF EXISTING (FROM PG. 36)

(This illustration is a continuation of the one in Session 4, pg. 21. The changes in this illustration will show what happened after the fall.)

5 (The right side of the illustration is explained in Session 4, pg. 21.) Before the fall, Adam and Eve's ultimate purpose was to glorify God. After the fall, their purpose changed. Because they no longer contained God's life, they could not glorify God (blocked).

6 Being blocked from their original purpose, they found a new purpose in honoring and glorifying themselves.

7 The "me" in the illustration is referred to as the "old self" in the Bible (Rom. 6:6; Eph. 4:22).

1 Adam and Eve were separated from God. God did not change. Adam and Eve changed. They separated themselves from God by their choice that resulted in acts of disobedience (sins).

8 The old self attempted to achieve honor. The purpose of honoring self was to build self-esteem in order to "feel" good with the hope of being satisfied.

2 Without God's life, their deepest needs went unmet. Therefore, they tried to meet their needs through their own power and resources. Instead of depending on God to meet their needs and living from the inside-out, they now had to live from the outside-in.

9 Ultimately, every attempt to get satisfaction apart from God's life does not work. The disappointment leads to rethinking ways to achieve satisfaction.

4 After the Fall, their broken system of attempting to achieve life could be described as a system of "choice." The knowledge of good and evil replaced God's life.

3 Adam and Eve felt worth-less as a result of their needs going unmet.

ILLUSTRATION: HOW FLESH IS PROGRAMMED (FROM PG. 40)

(This illustration is a continuation of the one in Session 6, pg. 36. The changes in this illustration will show how flesh is programmed through re-thinking.)

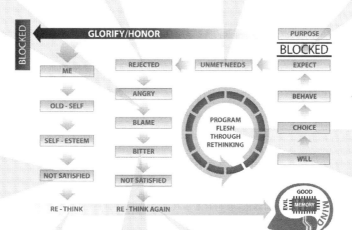

5 When our needs are not met, we experience rejection.

4 A blocked purpose results in an expectation not being met, which means a need is not met.

3 Often we find that the plans to achieve satisfaction are blocked by something or someone.

6 As we think on the rejection, we feel hurt and become angry. In our hurt and anger, we usually blame others to feel better about ourselves.

1 The goal of flesh is to get our needs met and be satisfied apart from God. We can set goals and achieve them and still not be satisfied nor experience any lasting satisfaction.

9 By repeating what gives us temporary satisfaction and discontinuing what doesn't, we are programming our flesh.

2 In our dissatisfaction, we re-think our strategies to meet our needs and find satisfaction apart from God.

7 Unresolved anger turns into bitterness, and results in us being unsatisfied again.

8 As we continue to re-think what to do next, we make new choices. We behave in an attempt to meet our expectations of satisfying ourselves - striving to achieve this satisfaction.

ILLUSTRATION: CONFIDENCE BASED FLESH (FROM PG. 42)

Significant people send us positive messages as we grow up.

Examples: "You are so cute." "Great job getting all A's!" "I am so proud of you for hitting that home run."

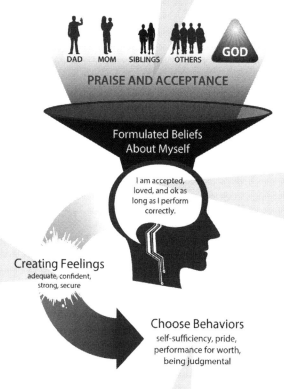

DAD   MOM   SIBLINGS   OTHERS   **GOD**

PRAISE AND ACCEPTANCE

Formulated Beliefs About Myself

I am accepted, loved, and ok as long as I perform correctly.

Creating Feelings
adequate, confident, strong, secure

Choose Behaviors
self-sufficiency, pride, performance for worth, being judgmental

2

These positive messages lead us to formulate positive or confident beliefs about ourselves such as "I am accepted, loved, and okay as long as I perform correctly and hear praise."

3

These positive beliefs create feelings that are pleasant.

Examples: adequate, confident, strong, secure, positive, hopeful, enthusiastic, happy, etc.

4

We choose behaviors based on these beliefs we have formulated about ourselves.

Examples: self-sufficiency, performance for worth ("I MUST do this right."), or being judgmental ("People who fail or make bad decisions are weak.")

ILLUSTRATION: SHAME BASED FLESH (FROM PG. 43)

1 Significant people send us negative messages as we grow up. The intent of the message may or may not be to reject, but what matters is that we perceive or interpret it as rejection.

Examples: "You are getting so chubby." "You will never amount to anything." "Why can't you get good grades like your sister?"

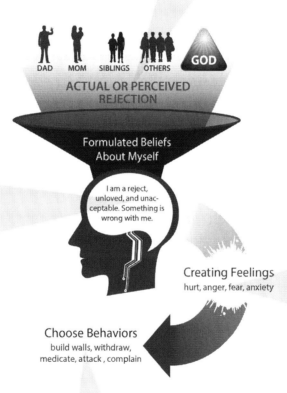

2 These negative messages lead us to formulate negative or shameful beliefs about ourselves such as "I am a reject, unloved, and unacceptable," or "Something is wrong with me."

3 These negative beliefs create feelings that are unpleasant or burdensome.

Examples: hurt, anger, fear, anxiety, pessimistic, weak, paranoid, etc.

4 We choose behaviors based on these beliefs we have formulated about ourselves.

Examples: build walls ("I won't let anyone in."), withdraw ("I am better off by myself."), medicate (addictions), attack ("I will hurt you before you hurt me."), complain ("I am a victim." "I never catch a break." "It is the other person's fault.")

ILLUSTRATION: PLACED SPIRITUALLY INTO CHRIST (FROM PG. 50)

(This illustration is a continuation of the one in Session 6, pg. 35. This illustration picks up at the incarnation of Jesus Christ.)

1 God, in the person of Jesus Christ, entered into the time line of human history. He was born of a virgin and took on flesh and blood.

5 Spiritually we ascend into heaven with Him and are now resting in Christ.

3 At the end of His earthly ministry, Jesus willingly gave up His earthly life, was crucified, died, was buried, was resurrected, and ascended into heaven.

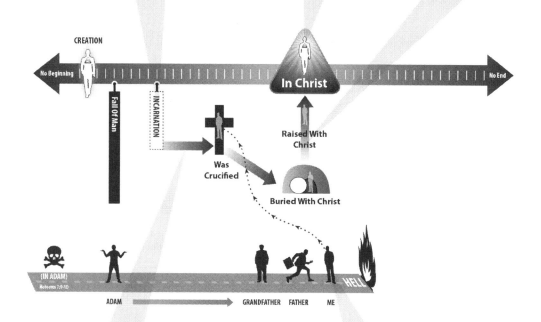

2 Jesus was the "second Adam." Like Adam, prior to the fall, he possessed God's life and nature. Unlike Adam, Jesus did not disobey. He lived a sinless life from cradle to grave in total dependence on His Heavenly Father.

4 At the moment we believe in and embrace Jesus' death and resurrection, God takes us spiritually from Adam's lineage and places us into Christ where we are crucified, buried, and resurrected to new life. We are re-birthed by the Holy Spirit in the likeness and holiness of Jesus Christ which results in an entirely new identity as a child of God.

ILLUSTRATION: LIFE RESTORED BY JESUS CHRIST (FROM PG. 55)

(This illustration is first introduced in Session 2, pg. 9. It is continued in Session 6, pg. 34.)

3 As presented in Session 8, God's solution to "Problem #2" (our "old self" or "sin nature") was to crucify (put to death) the "old self" with Christ.

4 At our co-crucifixion with Christ, God replaced (exchanged) our old sinful nature in Adam with a new nature that is Christ's nature. This new creation is often referred to as a saint and a child of God, which is now our new identity. The new saint is free from the old sinful nature and can live out of the freedom of being in Christ. This is inside-out living.

2 At the moment of salvation, the Holy Spirit enters and indwells us, giving us God's life. We are sealed forever by the Holy Spirit as a sign of God's authority, our belonging, and the security that we will always live together with Him.

1 As presented in Session 8, God's solution to "Problem #1" (humanity's separation caused by acts of disobedience (sins)) was through the sacrificial death of Christ. Jesus' shed blood has provided God's forgiveness, removing the barrier and restoring intimate fellowship.

5 Our soul, which merely existed, is now also brought to life, becoming a "living soul" who can express the believer's new nature in Christ. God's life now interacts with our soul renewing our thoughts, capturing our emotions, and directing our will. (This concept will be addressed in "The Believer's Battle," Session 13.)

6 "Flesh" and the law of sin remain. (This will be addressed in "The Believer's Battle," Session 14.)

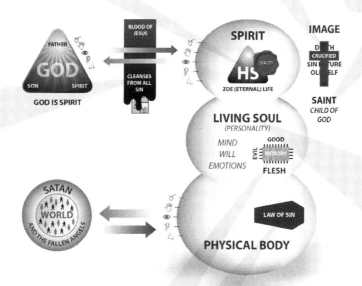

ILLUSTRATION: GOD'S PROVISION IN JESUS CHRIST (FROM PG. 56)

(This illustration is first introduced in Session 3, pg. 15. It is continued in Session 4, pg. 21, and shown as a broken system of existing in Session 6, pg. 36.)

6 Since God eradicated both our sins and our sin nature, we are now able to fulfill our original purpose of glorifying God. Living out of God's life and looking to Him to meet our needs, we express His life to others, gifting them love and thus glorifying God.

1 As seen in Session 8, God's solution to humanity's separation caused by our acts of disobedience (sins-"Problem #1") was through the sacrificial death of Christ. Jesus' shed blood has provided God's forgiveness, removing the barrier and restoring a personal relationship with intimate fellowship.

5 God replaced (exchanged) the old self with a new nature that is Christ's nature.

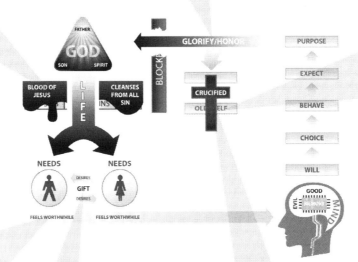

2 Now we are able to get our needs met from God. When we experience His complete provision, we feel worthwhile.

4 As also seen in Session 8, God's solution to "Problem #2" (our "old self" or sin nature) was to crucify (put to death) the "old self" with Christ. At the moment of belief, we receive both forgiveness of all sins and co-crucifixion of our sin nature.

3 Being content and fulfilled in getting our needs met from God alone, we are now free to gift to others desires such as love and respect without needing to receive anything in return.

ILLUSTRATION: THE BATTLE FOR THE MIND (FROM PG. 87)

(This illustration is first introduced in Session 2, p. 9, where it shows the design of man. It is continued in Session 6, p. 34, to show man after the fall. Finally in Session 9, p. 55, this illustration is developed to show how God has restored us.)

1 We were designed to operate according to the law of the mind, which naturally receives God's truth (Rom. 7:22) (Session 4, p. 20, sub-section, "WHAT ARE THE MECHANICS OF GLORIFYING GOD?"). After the Fall, humanity operated according to the law of sin. As new creations, we are no longer slaves to sin, but our nature is to operate in the law of the mind.

2 God through the Holy Spirit places truthful thoughts into our minds.

3 The demonic forces and the world can also introduce lies into our minds. These lies often come at times that intersect with desires of the flesh.

5 The raging war inside a believer is between lies and the truth. The lies are launched by Satan and fueled by the desires of the flesh. The truth is provided by God in accordance with the desires of the Spirit.

7 We can choose to believe the lie, walk (think and behave) "after the flesh", and live from the outside-in.

8 Or, we can submit to the Holy Spirit by choosing to believe the truth, take the thoughts (lies) captive, trash the lies, walk in obedience to the Spirit, and live from the inside-out.

6 Each battle ends when we make a choice with our will.

4 These evil thoughts are like flaming missiles. When they hit us, they will light a fire in our emotions if they are not put out. The fiery thoughts do not belong to us unless we embrace them.

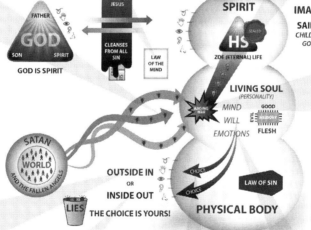

ILLUSTRATION: TARGETING LIES WITH THE TRUTH (FROM PG. 88)

The bullets on the sides represent truths relating to our identity in Christ. As we are attacked with lies from the enemy, the Spirit provides the appropriate truth (bullet) loaded into our mind. By faith we eliminate the lie, replacing it with the truth of our identity.

TAKE AIM AT THE LIES. YOUR AMMUNITION IS THE TRUTH.

"For though we walk in the flesh, we do not war according to the flesh, for the weapons of our warfare are not of the flesh, but divinely powerful for the destruction of fortresses. We are destroying speculations and every lofty thing raised up against the knowledge of God, and we are taking every thought captive to the obedience of Christ," 2 Corinthians 10:3-5

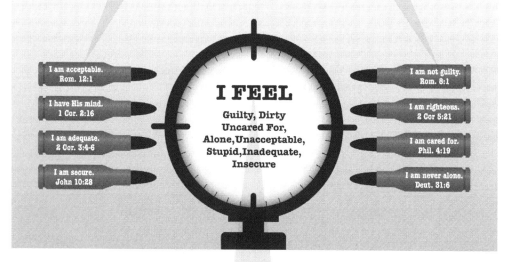

Sometimes it is hard to discern or identify the lies that are launched at us (or that we are believing). The circle represents a scope of a rifle. Just as a scope helps us aim at a target, so too our feelings help us zero in on the lies. The feelings listed (guilty, dirty, uncared for, etc.), are indicators of what we might be believing about ourselves (I am guilty, I am dirty, I am uncared for, etc.).

ILLUSTRATION: MARRIED TO MR. LAW OR MR. GRACE? (FROM PG. 128)

(This illustration is taken from Romans 7:1-6.)

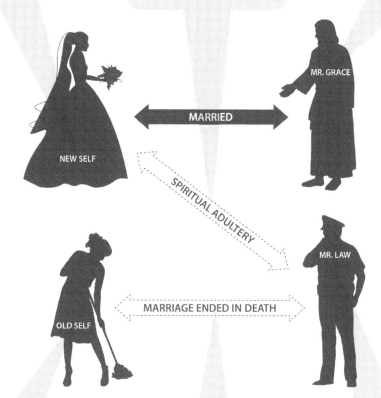

4 We are now a new creation and are married to another – Mr. Grace (Christ).

6 When a woman who is married goes to live with another man while her husband is alive, she is committing adultery. When a believer tries to attain God's acceptance through self effort (operate under a law system), he/she is committing spiritual adultery.

5 Mr. Grace provides for everything Mr. Law could not. The grace of God gives us the desire to do what is right. His law of love is written on our hearts. Christ's life in us is the grace we need to live the Christian life of love.

MR. GRACE

NEW SELF

MARRIED

SPIRITUAL ADULTERY

MR. LAW

OLD SELF

MARRIAGE ENDED IN DEATH

1 In Adam, we (old self) were "married" to the Law.

3 Since Mr. Law cannot die, in Christ we were made to die to Mr. Law.

2 Mr. Law is good and perfect, and he demands perfection. However, he does nothing to assist his spouse to be perfect. A person under the Law is left to his/her own resources and performance to try to meet the standard placed upon him/her.

ILLUSTRATION: TWO SYSTEMS OF LIVING (FROM PG. 129)

(This illustration shows the difference between behavior generated from God's life within and behavior produced from self-effort in an attempt to be good and do what is right.)

1 "Life" is God's life. His life is dynamic from moment to moment.

2 As Adam and Eve lived in relationship with God, they had the freedom to choose to live out of His life in them.

3 Their choices led to behaviors that reflected their dynamic relationship with God. They were living from the inside-out. They experienced freedom because their choices were made out of God's life rather than trying to produce life. They operated under a receiving system of grace whereby they received from God and expressed His life in them to each other.

4 When Adam and Eve sinned, they lost God's life and fell from this receiving system of living.

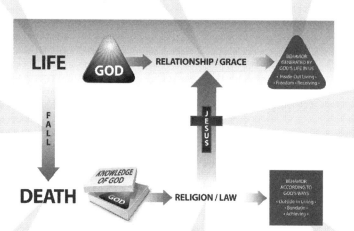

8 Jesus met all the requirements of God's law and fulfilled the law's purpose. By His grace, He set us free and restored life in us by the Spirit. Through Jesus we can have a personal relationship with God and live from the inside-out, expressing His life in us to those around us.

5 The absence of God's life is spiritual death. Since Adam and Eve were still physically alive, they were just existing. In Adam, all humanity is born spiritually dead.

6 Having a knowledge of God without an empowering personal relationship with God can lead to religion. Religion is made up of laws intended to regulate a person's behavior in order to produce righteous living.

7 In this achieving system, behaviors that are supposed to be good or godly are still sinful because they are not produced from God's life. They are only a distorted copy. Keeping the law is an attempt to gain God's acceptance and feel good about ourselves. This system is a stagnant way of existing that can be described as outside-in living. Achieving without God's empowerment results in slavery to sin and bondage to the Law.

ILLUSTRATION: SHARING AND EQUIPPING IN RELATIONSHIPS (FROM PG. 143)

1

God exists in relationship (see pg. 3) and indwells us with His Holy Spirit (see p. 54-55).

4

The Holy Spirit also directs us into intentional relationships with others who have placed their faith and trust in Jesus. All believers are at various stages in their spiritual growth (Session 13).

5

The line from left to right illustrates the journey of a person from darkness to light and from immaturity to maturity.

2

He designed us to intentionally share life with others in relationship. Every point of contact inside a relationship provides us with an opportunity to express the life and love of God. As we go along our journey of life, we meet and interact with both unbelievers and believers.

3

With unbelievers, we have the opportunity to show them God's love and then give witness as to the reason for our hope, faith, peace and love. As we share life, we invite them to accept God's free gift of life through Jesus (evangelism).

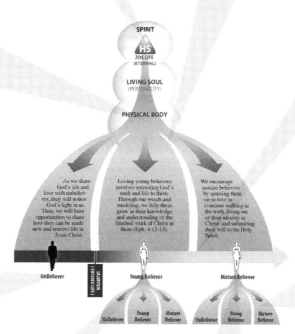

8

The believers that we equip now seek the Holy Spirit's guidance to intentionally share life with others in relationship and either invite the unbeliever to accept God's free gift of life through Jesus (evangelism), equip young (new or immature) believers, or encourage and spur on mature believers.

6

Journeying in life with young (new or immature) believers gives us the chance to equip them for life by helping them grow in their knowledge and understanding of the finished work of Christ in them (discipleship).

7

When we encounter mature believers, we have the privilege to encourage them by spurring them on in love to continue walking in the truth, living out of their identity in Christ and submitting their will to the Holy Spirit.

ABOUT THE AUTHORS

This "Living IN Jesus" study has been written by the combined effort of the counseling and coaching staff at Christian Families Today (CFT). CFT exists to educate and encourage men, women, and children in building biblically healthy lives and families. The truths found in this study are distilled from our 10-month Advanced Discipleship Training course and from close to four decades of experience in counseling and coaching individuals to live out of Christ's life. CFT is a member of Network 220 (www.network220.org). Some diagrams and content in this publication have been adapted from Network 220 conference materials. Network 220 (named after Galatians 2:20) is an international network of churches, counseling ministries, and training ministries who are committed to the life-changing message of our new identity and life in Jesus Christ.

ADDITIONAL RESOURCES

((PODCAST))

Enjoy weekly conversations with CFT staff on what it means to live a grace-filled life with Jesus at the center.

www.CFTMinistry.org/Podcast/

ARE YOU LEADING A LIVING IN JESUS STUDY?

GET THE EQUIPPER'S GUIDE AT
amazon.com

TO FURTHER EQUIP THE LIFE EQUIPPER, THE FOLLOWING ARE AVAILABLE:

Grow in Grace Seminar: an expanded teaching of Romans 5-8 which sets forth a believer's identification with Christ in His death, burial, and resurrection. Through understanding how to appropriate one's identification in Christ, believers not only begin to understand the Exchanged Life, but also learn how to bring life's trials and tribulations to resolution. This seminar is presented quarterly at Christian Families Today's office in Newnan, GA.

Advanced Discipleship Training (ADT): provides a deeper and more comprehensive understanding of The Exchanged Life through teaching a believer's identification in Christ, learning how to build biblically healthy relationships based upon a believer's identification in Christ and learning how a believer can effectively share his or her identification in Christ with others. This training is conducted at Christian Families Today's office in Newnan, GA and internationally through the internet.

For more information on these opportunities and additional resources, visit our website at:

www.ChristianFamiliesToday.org

Made in the USA
Columbia, SC
27 February 2022

56948183R00098